Microsoft®
Access 2000
Simplified™

IDG's **3-D Visual™** Series

IDG BOOKS *From* **maranGraphics™**

IDG Books Worldwide, Inc.
An International Data Group Company
Foster City, CA • Indianapolis • Chicago • New York

Microsoft® Access 2000 Simplified™

Published by
IDG Books Worldwide, Inc.
An International Data Group Company
919 E. Hillsdale Blvd., Suite 400
Foster City, CA 94404
(650) 655-3000

Library of Congress Catalog Card No.: 99-62447
ISBN: 0-7645-6058-1
Printed in the United States of America
10 9 8 7 6 5 4 3 2 1

Distributed in the United States by IDG Books Worldwide, Inc.
Distributed by CDG Books Canada Inc. for Canada; by Transworld Publishers Limited in the United Kingdom; by IDG Norge Books for Norway; by IDG Sweden Books for Sweden; by Woodslane Pty. Ltd. for Australia; by Woodslane (NZ) Ltd. for New Zealand; by TransQuest Publishers Pte Ltd. for Singapore, Malaysia, Thailand, Indonesia, and Hong Kong; by ICG Muse, Inc. for Japan; by Norma Comunicaciones S.A. for Colombia; by Intersoft for South Africa; by Le Monde en Tique for France; by International Thomson Publishing for Germany, Austria and Switzerland; by Distribuidora Cuspide for Argentina; by Livraria Cultura for Brazil; by Ediciones ZETA S.C.R. Ltda. for Peru; by WS Computer Publishing Corporation, Inc., for the Philippines; by Contemporanea de Ediciones for Venezuela; by Express Computer Distributors for the Caribbean and West Indies; by Micronesia Media Distributor, Inc. for Micronesia; by Grupo Editorial Norma S.A. for Guatemala; by Chips Computadoras S.A. de C.V. for Mexico; by Editorial Norma de Panama S.A. for Panama; by American Bookshops for Finland. Authorized Sales Agent: Anthony Rudkin Associates for the Middle East and North Africa.
For corporate orders, please call maranGraphics at 800-469-6616.
For general information on IDG Books Worldwide's books in the U.S., please call our Consumer Customer Service department at 800-762-2974.
For reseller information, including discounts and premium sales, please call our Reseller Customer Service department at 800-434-3422.
For information on where to purchase IDG Books Worldwide's books outside the U.S., please contact our International Sales department at 317-596-5530 or fax 317-596-5692.
For consumer information on foreign language translations, please contact our Customer Service department at 1-800-434-3422, fax 317-596-5692, or e-mail rights@idgbooks.com.
For information on licensing foreign or domestic rights, please phone 1-650-655-3109.
For sales inquiries and special prices for bulk quantities, please contact our Sales department at 650-655-3200.
For information on using IDG Books Worldwide's books in the classroom or for ordering examination copies, please contact our Educational Sales department at 800-434-2086 or fax 317-596-5499.
For press review copies, author interviews, or other publicity information, please contact our Public Relations department at 650-655-3000 or fax 650-655-3299.
For authorization to photocopy items for corporate, personal, or educational use, please contact maranGraphics at 800-469-6616.

Trademark Acknowledgments

Permission

The 3-D illustrations are the copyright of maranGraphics, Inc.

U.S. Corporate Sales	U.S. Trade Sales
Contact maranGraphics at (800) 469-6616 or fax (905) 890-9434.	Contact IDG Books at (800) 434-3422 or (650) 655-3000.

ABOUT IDG BOOKS WORLDWIDE

Welcome to the world of IDG Books Worldwide.

IDG Books Worldwide, Inc., is a subsidiary of International Data Group, the world's largest publisher of computer-related information and the leading global provider of information services on information technology. IDG was founded more than 30 years ago by Patrick J. McGovern and now employs more than 9,000 people worldwide. IDG publishes more than 290 computer publications in over 75 countries. More than 90 million people read one or more IDG publications each month.

Launched in 1990, IDG Books Worldwide is today the #1 publisher of best-selling computer books in the United States. We are proud to have received eight awards from the Computer Press Association in recognition of editorial excellence and three from Computer Currents' First Annual Readers' Choice Awards. Our best-selling ...For Dummies® series has more than 50 million copies in print with translations in 31 languages. IDG Books Worldwide, through a joint venture with IDG's Hi-Tech Beijing, became the first U.S. publisher to publish a computer book in the People's Republic of China. In record time, IDG Books Worldwide has become the first choice for millions of readers around the world who want to learn how to better manage their businesses.

Our mission is simple: Every one of our books is designed to bring extra value and skill-building instructions to the reader. Our books are written by experts who understand and care about our readers. The knowledge base of our editorial staff comes from years of experience in publishing, education, and journalism — experience we use to produce books to carry us into the new millennium. In short, we care about books, so we attract the best people. We devote special attention to details such as audience, interior design, use of icons, and illustrations. And because we use an efficient process of authoring, editing, and desktop publishing our books electronically, we can spend more time ensuring superior content and less time on the technicalities of making books.

You can count on our commitment to deliver high-quality books at competitive prices on topics you want to read about. At IDG Books Worldwide, we continue in the IDG tradition of delivering quality for more than 30 years. You'll find no better book on a subject than one from IDG Books Worldwide.

John Kilcullen
Chairman and CEO
IDG Books Worldwide, Inc.

Steven Berkowitz
President and Publisher
IDG Books Worldwide, Inc.

Eighth Annual Computer Press Awards 1992 | Ninth Annual Computer Press Awards 1993 | Tenth Annual Computer Press Awards 1994 | Eleventh Annual Computer Press Awards 1995

maranGraphics is a family-run business
located near Toronto, Canada.

At **maranGraphics**, we believe in producing great computer books–one book at a time.

Each maranGraphics book uses the award-winning communication process that we have been developing over the last 25 years. Using this process, we organize screen shots, text and illustrations in a way that makes it easy for you to learn new concepts and tasks.

We spend hours deciding the best way to perform each task, so you don't have to! Our clear, easy-to-follow screen shots and instructions walk you through each task from beginning to end.

Our detailed illustrations go hand-in-hand with the text to help reinforce the information. Each illustration is a labor of love–some take up to a week to draw!

We want to thank you for purchasing what we feel are the best computer books money can buy. We hope you enjoy using this book as much as we enjoyed creating it!

Sincerely,

The Maran Family

Please visit us on the web at:
www.maran.com

Credits

Author:
Ruth Maran

Copy Editors:
Cathy Benn
Jill Maran

Project Manager:
Judy Maran

Editing & Screen Captures:
Raquel Scott
Janice Boyer
Michelle Kirchner
James Menzies
Frances Lea
Emmet Mellow

Layout Designers:
Jamie Bell
Treena Lees

Illustrators:
Russ Marini
Jamie Bell
Peter Grecco
Sean Johannesen
Steven Schaerer

Screen Artist & Revisions:
Jimmy Tam

Indexer:
Raquel Scott

Post Production:
Robert Maran

Editorial Support:
Michael Roney

Acknowledgments

Thanks to the dedicated staff of maranGraphics, including
Jamie Bell, Cathy Benn, Janice Boyer, Francisco Ferreira,
Peter Grecco, Jenn Hillman, Sean Johannesen, Michelle Kirchner,
Wanda Lawrie, Frances Lea, Treena Lees, Jill Maran, Judy Maran,
Maxine Maran, Robert Maran, Sherry Maran, Russ Marini,
Emmet Mellow, James Menzies, Stacey Morrison, Roben Ponce,
Steven Schaerer, Raquel Scott, Jimmy Tam, Roxanne Van Damme,
Paul Whitehead and Kelleigh Wing.

Finally, to Richard Maran who originated the easy-to-use
graphic format of this guide. Thank you for your
inspiration and guidance.

Table of Contents

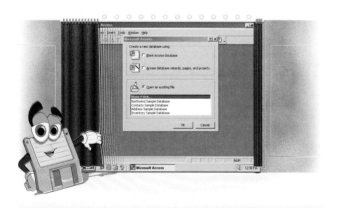

CHAPTER 4

EDIT TABLES

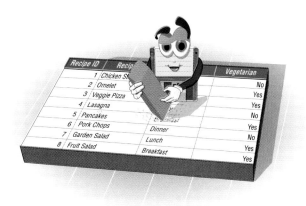

CHAPTER 5

DESIGN TABLES

Table of Contents

CHAPTER 6

ESTABLISH RELATIONSHIPS

CHAPTER 7

CREATE FORMS

CHAPTER 8

FIND DATA

CHAPTER 9

CREATE QUERIES

PRINT INFORMATION

CHAPTER 10

CREATE REPORTS

CHAPTER 12

ACCESS AND THE INTERNET

CHAPTER 1

GETTING STARTED

Wondering where to start with Microsoft Access 2000? This chapter will show you the way.

Microsoft Access is a database program that allows you to store and manage large collections of information.

Access provides you with all the tools you need to create an efficient and effective database.

WHY WOULD I USE A DATABASE?

Personal Uses

Many people use databases to store personal information such as addresses, recipes, music collections and wine lists. Using a database to store and organize information is much more efficient than using sheets of paper or index cards.

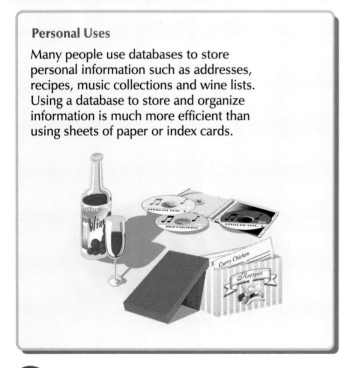

Business Uses

Companies use databases to store information such as mailing lists, customer orders, expenses, inventory and payroll. A database can help a company effectively review, update and analyze information that constantly changes.

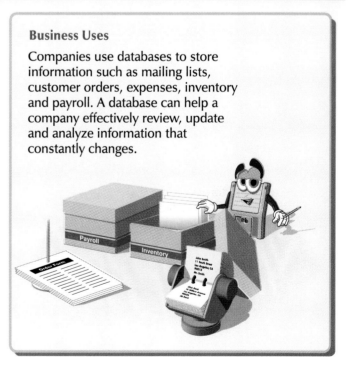

DATABASE APPLICATIONS

Store Information

A database stores and manages a collection of information related to a particular subject or purpose. You can efficiently add, update, view and organize the information stored in a database.

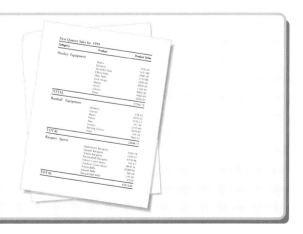

Find Information

You can instantly locate information of interest in a database. For example, you can find all customers with the last name "Smith". You can also perform more advanced searches, such as finding all customers living in California who purchased more than $100 of your product last year.

Analyze and Print Information

You can perform calculations on the information in a database to help you make quick, accurate and informed decisions. You can neatly present the information in professionally designed reports.

PARTS OF A DATABASE

A database consists of tables, forms, queries and reports.

Tables

A table stores information about a specific topic, such as a mailing list. You can have one or more tables in a database. A table consists of fields and records.

Address ID	First Name	Last Name	Address	City	State/Province	Postal Code
1	Jim	Schmith	258 Linton Ave.	New York	NY	10010
2	Brenda	Petterson	50 Tree Lane	Boston	MA	02117
3	Todd	Talbot	68 Cracker Ave.	San Francisco	CA	94110
4	Chuck	Dean	47 Crosby Ave.	Las Vegas	NV	89116
5	Melanie	Robinson	26 Arnold Cres.	Jacksonville	FL	32256
6	Susan	Hughes	401 Idon Dr.	Nashville	TN	37243
7	Allen	Toppins	10 Heldon St.	Atlanta	GA	30375
8	Greg	Kilkenny	36 Buzzard St.	Boston	MA	02118
9	Jason	Marcuson	15 Bizzo Pl.	New York	NY	10020
10	Jim	Martin	890 Apple St.	San Diego	CA	92121

Field

A field is a specific category of information, such as the first names of all your customers.

Record

A record is a collection of information about one person, place or thing, such as the name and address of one customer.

Forms

Forms provide a quick way to view, enter and change information in a database by presenting information in an attractive, easy-to-use format. Forms usually display one record at a time and display boxes that clearly show you where to enter information.

Queries

Queries allow you to find information of interest in a database. You can enter criteria in a query to specify what information you want to find. For example, you can create a query to find all customers who live in California.

Reports

Reports are professional-looking documents that summarize data in a database. You can perform calculations in a report to help you analyze your data. For example, you can create a report that displays the total sales for each product.

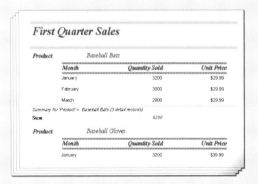

PLAN A DATABASE

You should take the time to plan your database. A well-planned database ensures that you will be able to perform tasks efficiently and accurately.

Determine the Purpose of the Database

Decide what information you want your database to store and how you plan to use the information. If other people will use the database, you should consult with them to determine their needs.

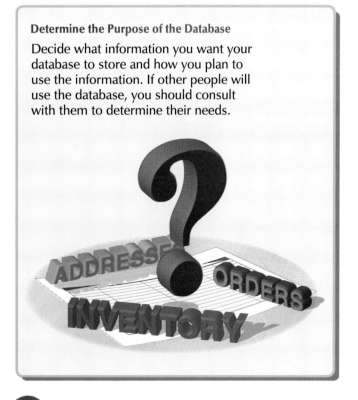

Determine the Tables You Need

Gather all the information you want to store in your database and then divide the information into separate tables. A table should contain information for only one subject.

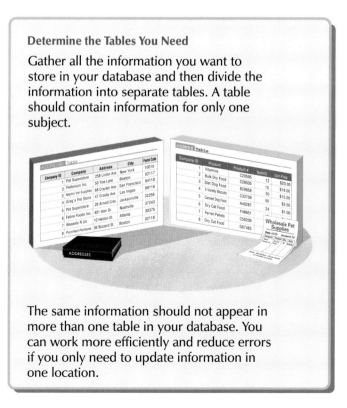

The same information should not appear in more than one table in your database. You can work more efficiently and reduce errors if you only need to update information in one location.

Determine the Fields You Need

➤ Each field should relate directly to the subject of the table.

➤ Make sure you break down information into its smallest parts. For example, break down names into two fields called First Name and Last Name.

➤ Try to keep the number of fields in a table to a minimum. Tables with many fields increase the time it takes Access to process information.

Determine the Primary Key

A primary key is one or more fields that uniquely identifies each record in a table. Each table in a database should have a primary key. For example, the primary key in a table containing employee information can be the social security number for each employee.

Determine the Relationships Between Tables

Relationships between tables allow you to bring together related information in your database. You will usually relate the primary key in one table to a matching field in another table to form a relationship.

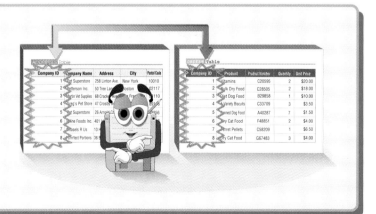

USING THE MOUSE

A mouse is a handheld device that lets you select and move items on your screen.

When you move the mouse on your desk, the mouse pointer on your screen moves in the same direction. The mouse pointer assumes different shapes, such as ▷ or I, depending on its location on your screen and the task you are performing.

Resting your hand on the mouse, use your thumb and two rightmost fingers to move the mouse on your desk. Use your two remaining fingers to press the mouse buttons.

MOUSE ACTIONS

Click

Press and release the left mouse button.

Double-click

Quickly press and release the left mouse button twice.

Right-click

Press and release the right mouse button.

Drag

Position the mouse pointer over an object on your screen and then press and hold down the left mouse button. Still holding down the button, move the mouse to where you want to place the object and then release the button.

10

START ACCESS

You can start Access to create a new database or work with a database you previously created.

START ACCESS

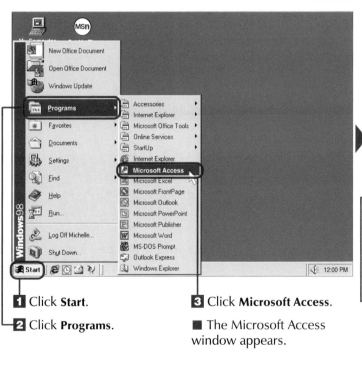

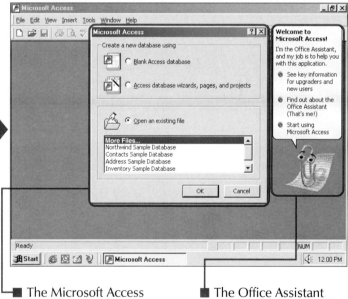

1 Click **Start**.

2 Click **Programs**.

3 Click **Microsoft Access**.

■ The Microsoft Access window appears.

■ The Microsoft Access dialog box appears each time you start Access, allowing you to create or open a database.

Note: To create a database, see page 12 or 18. To open a database, see page 28.

■ The Office Assistant welcome appears the first time you start Access.

Note: For information on the Office Assistant, see page 24.

CREATE A DATABASE USING THE DATABASE WIZARD

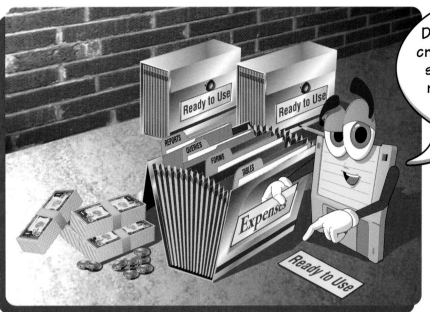

You can use the Database Wizard to help you create a database. The wizard saves you time by providing ready-to-use objects, such as tables, forms, queries and reports.

You can use the Database Wizard to create many types of databases, such as databases for contact management, expenses, inventory control and order entry.

CREATE A DATABASE USING THE DATABASE WIZARD

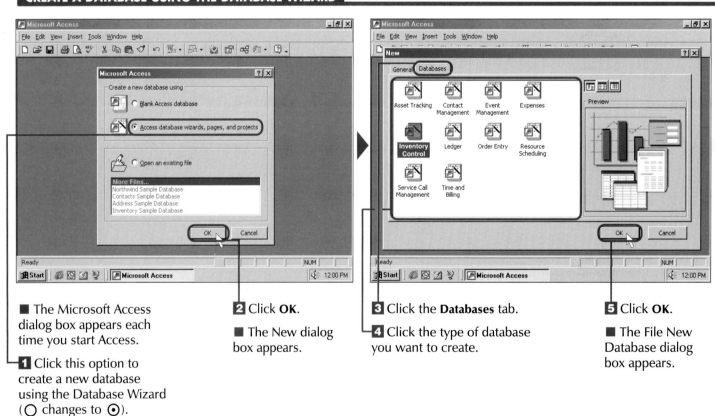

■ The Microsoft Access dialog box appears each time you start Access.

1 Click this option to create a new database using the Database Wizard (○ changes to ⊙).

2 Click **OK**.

■ The New dialog box appears.

3 Click the **Databases** tab.

4 Click the type of database you want to create.

5 Click **OK**.

■ The File New Database dialog box appears.

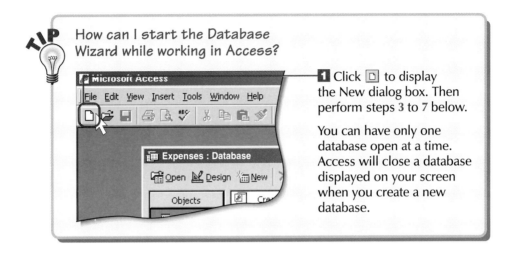

How can I start the Database
Wizard while working in Access?

1 Click □ to display
the New dialog box. Then
perform steps 3 to 7 below.

You can have only one
database open at a time.
Access will close a database
displayed on your screen
when you create a new
database.

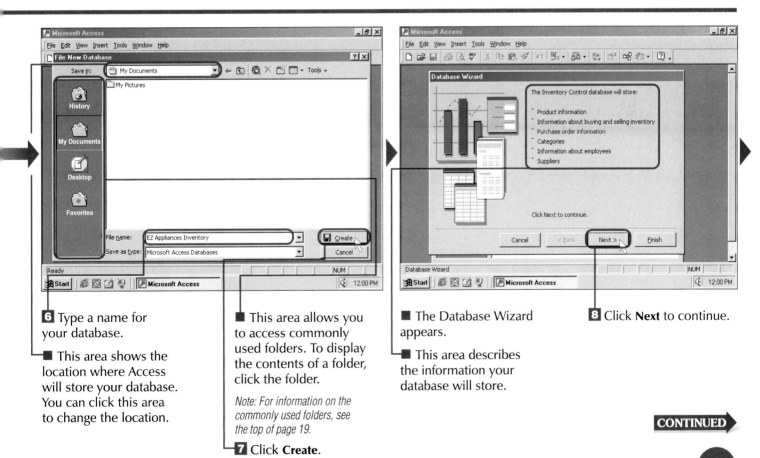

6 Type a name for
your database.

■ This area shows the
location where Access
will store your database.
You can click this area
to change the location.

■ This area allows you
to access commonly
used folders. To display
the contents of a folder,
click the folder.

*Note: For information on the
commonly used folders, see
the top of page 19.*

7 Click **Create**.

■ The Database Wizard
appears.

■ This area describes
the information your
database will store.

8 Click **Next** to continue.

CONTINUED

CREATE A DATABASE USING THE DATABASE WIZARD

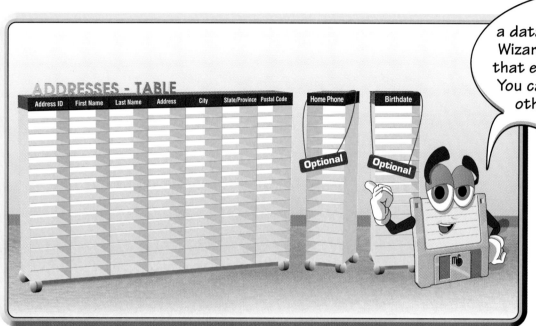

When creating a database, the Database Wizard displays the fields that each table will include. You can choose to include other optional fields.

A field is a specific category of information in a table, such as the last names of your customers.

CREATE A DATABASE USING THE DATABASE WIZARD (CONTINUED)

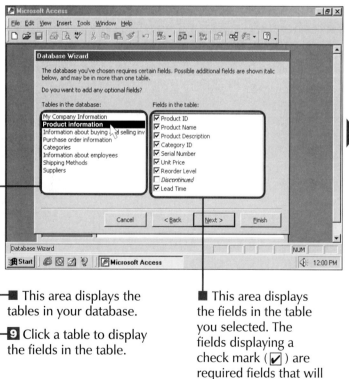

■ This area displays the tables in your database.

9 Click a table to display the fields in the table.

■ This area displays the fields in the table you selected. The fields displaying a check mark (☑) are required fields that will appear in the table. The other fields are optional.

10 To add an optional field to the table, click the box (☐) beside the field (☐ changes to ☑). Repeat this step for each optional field you want to add.

11 Click **Next** to continue.

14

Can I remove a required field from a table?

You can only remove a required field after you finish creating the database. To remove a field from a table, see page 49.

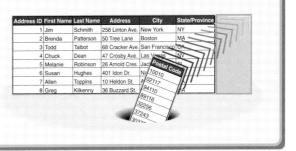

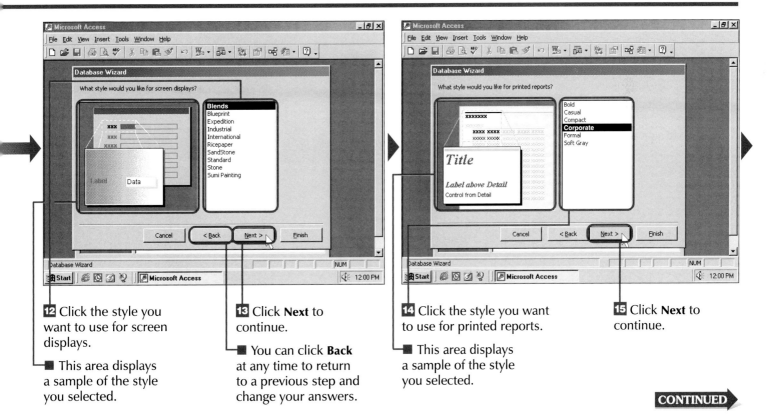

12 Click the style you want to use for screen displays.

■ This area displays a sample of the style you selected.

13 Click **Next** to continue.

■ You can click **Back** at any time to return to a previous step and change your answers.

14 Click the style you want to use for printed reports.

■ This area displays a sample of the style you selected.

15 Click **Next** to continue.

CONTINUED ▶

When you finish creating a database, Access displays a switchboard that can help you perform common tasks in the database.

CREATE A DATABASE USING THE DATABASE WIZARD (CONTINUED)

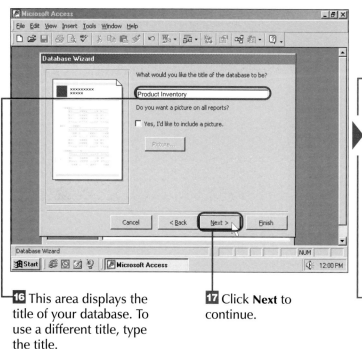

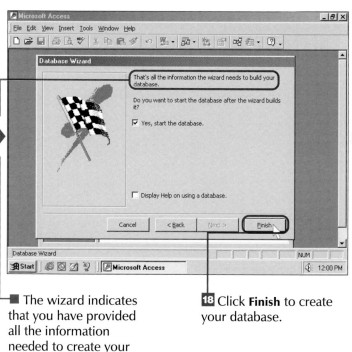

16 This area displays the title of your database. To use a different title, type the title.

17 Click **Next** to continue.

■ The wizard indicates that you have provided all the information needed to create your database.

18 Click **Finish** to create your database.

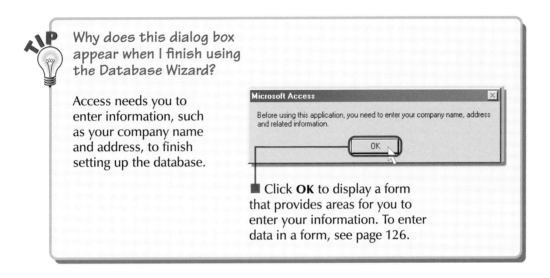

TIP

Why *does* this dialog box appear when I finish using the Database Wizard?

Access needs you to enter information, such as your company name and address, to finish setting up the database.

Microsoft Access

Before using this application, you need to enter your company name, address and related information.

OK

■ Click **OK** to display a form that provides areas for you to enter your information. To enter data in a form, see page 126.

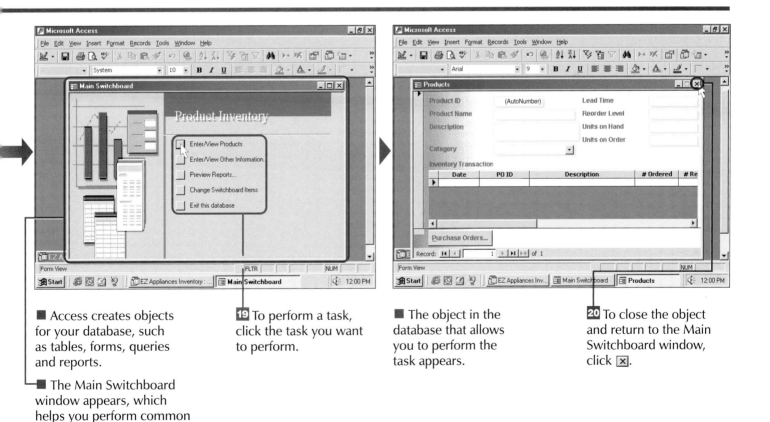

■ Access creates objects for your database, such as tables, forms, queries and reports.

■ The Main Switchboard window appears, which helps you perform common tasks in the database.

19 To perform a task, click the task you want to perform.

■ The object in the database that allows you to perform the task appears.

20 To close the object and return to the Main Switchboard window, click ⊠.

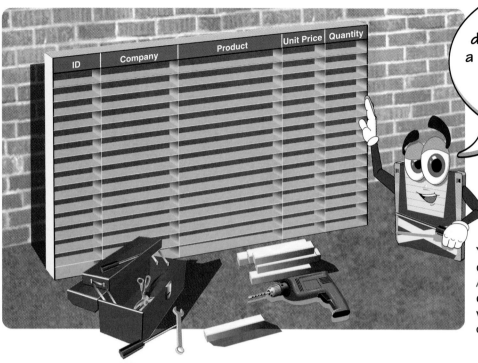

If you want to design your own database, you can create a blank database. Creating a blank database gives you the most flexibility and control.

You can have only one database open at a time. Access will close a database displayed on your screen when you create or open another database.

CREATE A BLANK DATABASE

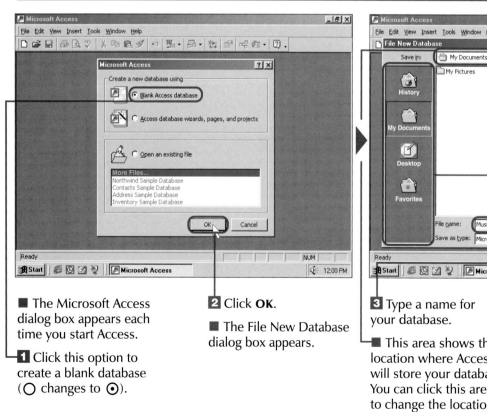

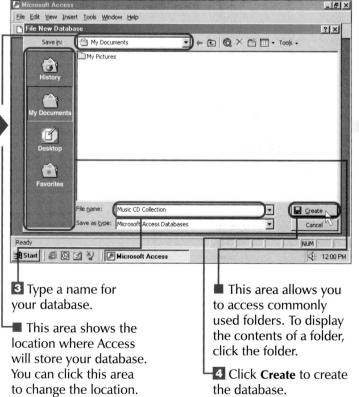

■ The Microsoft Access dialog box appears each time you start Access.

1 Click this option to create a blank database (○ changes to ⊙).

2 Click **OK**.

■ The File New Database dialog box appears.

3 Type a name for your database.

■ This area shows the location where Access will store your database. You can click this area to change the location.

■ This area allows you to access commonly used folders. To display the contents of a folder, click the folder.

4 Click **Create** to create the database.

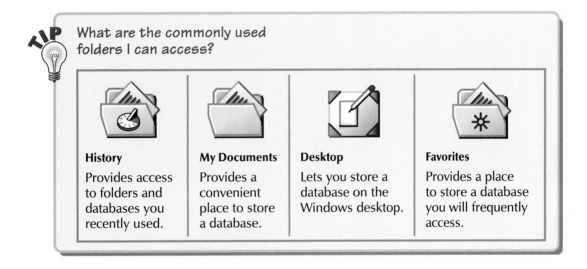

TIP

What are the commonly used folders I can access?

History
Provides access to folders and databases you recently used.

My Documents
Provides a convenient place to store a database.

Desktop
Lets you store a database on the Windows desktop.

Favorites
Provides a place to store a database you will frequently access.

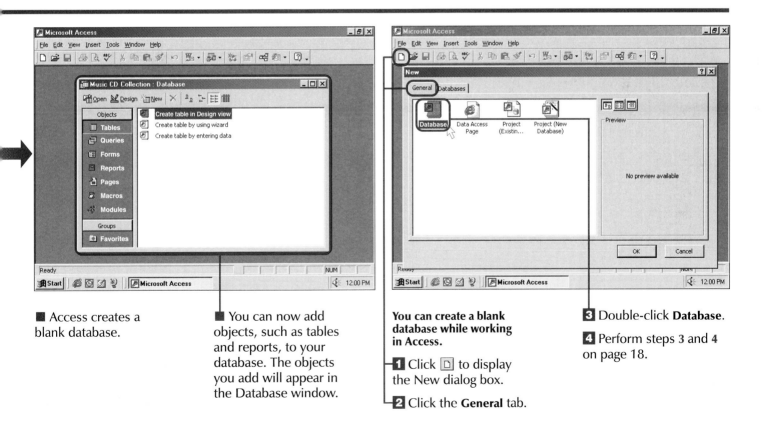

■ Access creates a blank database.

■ You can now add objects, such as tables and reports, to your database. The objects you add will appear in the Database window.

You can create a blank database while working in Access.

1 Click 🗋 to display the New dialog box.

2 Click the **General** tab.

3 Double-click **Database**.

4 Perform steps 3 and 4 on page 18.

You can select a command from a menu to perform a task. Each command performs a different task.

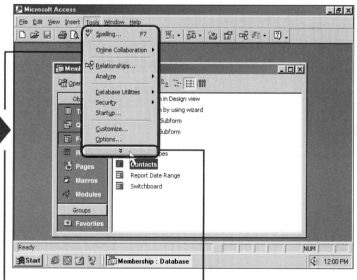

1 Click the name of the menu you want to display.

■ A short version of the menu appears, displaying the most commonly used commands.

2 To expand the menu and display all the commands, position the mouse ⌖ over ⌄.

Note: If you do not perform step 2, the expanded menu will automatically appear after a few seconds.

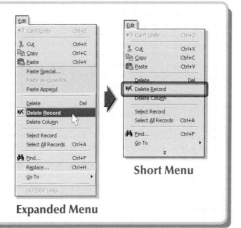

How can I make a command appear on the short version of a menu?

When you select a command from an expanded menu, Access automatically adds the command to the short version of the menu. The next time you display the short version of the menu, the command you selected will appear.

Short Menu

Expanded Menu

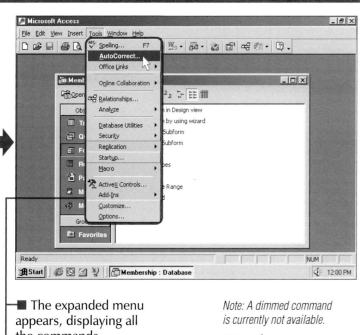

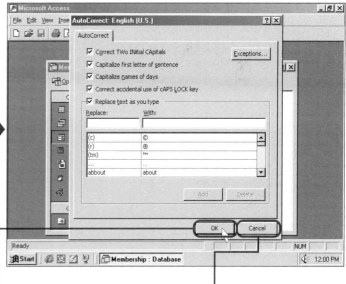

■ The expanded menu appears, displaying all the commands.

3 Click the command you want to use.

Note: A dimmed command is currently not available.

■ To close a menu without selecting a command, click outside the menu.

■ A dialog box appears if the command you selected displays three dots (...).

4 When you finish selecting options in the dialog box, click **OK** to confirm your changes.

■ To close the dialog box without making any changes, click **Cancel**.

SELECT COMMANDS USING TOOLBARS

A toolbar contains buttons that you can use to select commands. Each button allows you to perform a different task.

SELECT COMMANDS USING TOOLBARS

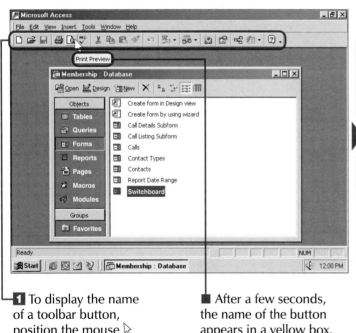

1 To display the name of a toolbar button, position the mouse over the button.

■ After a few seconds, the name of the button appears in a yellow box. The button name can help you determine the task the button performs.

2 To use a toolbar button to select a command, click the button.

22

When you finish using Access, you can exit the program.

You should exit all programs before turning off your computer.

EXIT ACCESS

1 Click **File**.

2 Click **Exit** to exit Access.

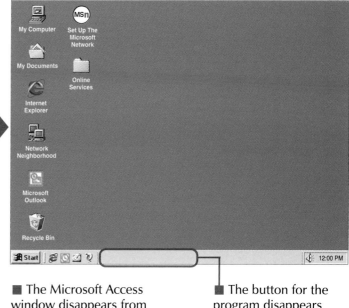

■ The Microsoft Access window disappears from your screen.

■ The button for the program disappears from the taskbar.

23

If you do not know how to perform a task, you can ask the Office Assistant for help.

GETTING HELP

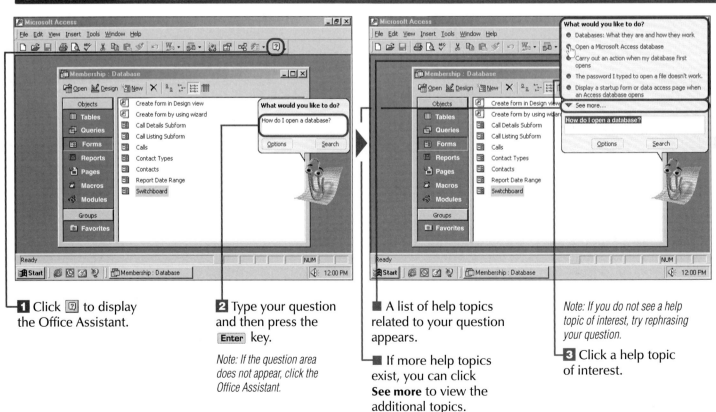

1 Click ⑦ to display the Office Assistant.

2 Type your question and then press the **Enter** key.

Note: If the question area does not appear, click the Office Assistant.

■ A list of help topics related to your question appears.

■ If more help topics exist, you can click **See more** to view the additional topics.

Note: If you do not see a help topic of interest, try rephrasing your question.

3 Click a help topic of interest.

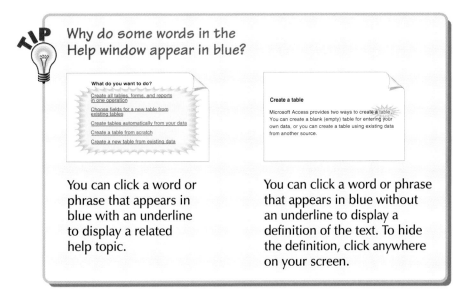

TIP

Why do some words in the Help window appear in blue?

You can click a word or phrase that appears in blue with an underline to display a related help topic.

You can click a word or phrase that appears in blue without an underline to display a definition of the text. To hide the definition, click anywhere on your screen.

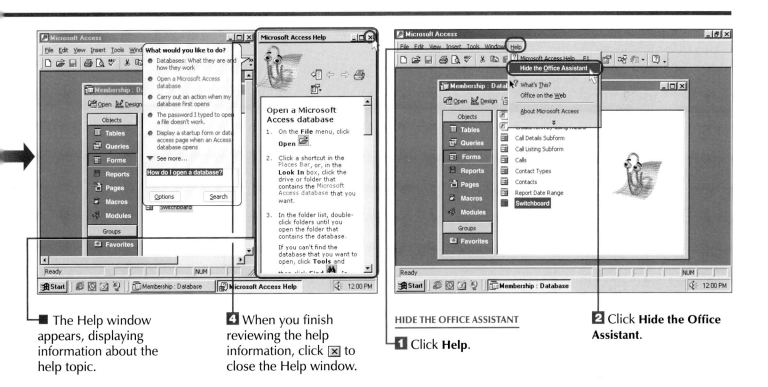

■ The Help window appears, displaying information about the help topic.

4 When you finish reviewing the help information, click ⊠ to close the Help window.

HIDE THE OFFICE ASSISTANT

1 Click **Help**.

2 Click **Hide the Office Assistant**.

CHAPTER 2

DATABASE BASICS

Are you ready to start working with your database? This chapter teaches you how.

You can open a database you previously created and display it on your screen. This lets you review and make changes to the database.

You can have only one database open at a time. Access will close a database displayed on your screen when you open another database.

OPEN A DATABASE

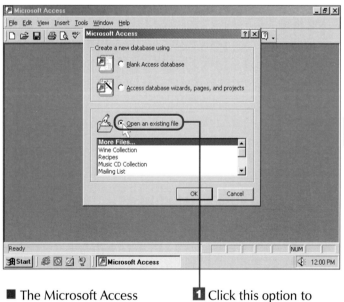

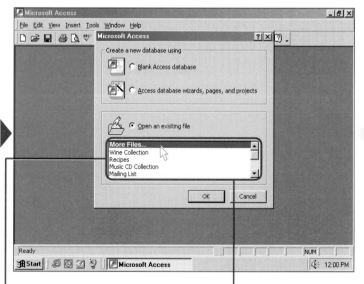

■ The Microsoft Access dialog box appears each time you start Access.

1 Click this option to open an existing database (○ changes to ⊙).

■ This area displays the names of the last databases you worked with. To open one of these databases, double-click the name of the database.

Note: The names of sample databases may also appear in the list.

2 If the database you want to open is not listed, double-click **More Files**.

■ The Open dialog box appears.

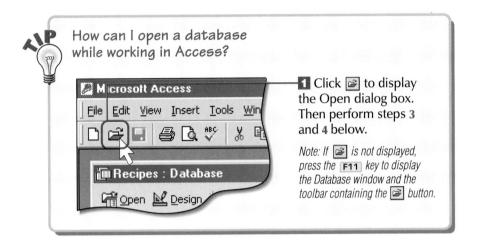

How can I open a database while working in Access?

1 Click 🖼 to display the Open dialog box. Then perform steps **3** and **4** below.

Note: If 🖼 is not displayed, press the `F11` *key to display the Database window and the toolbar containing the 🖼 button.*

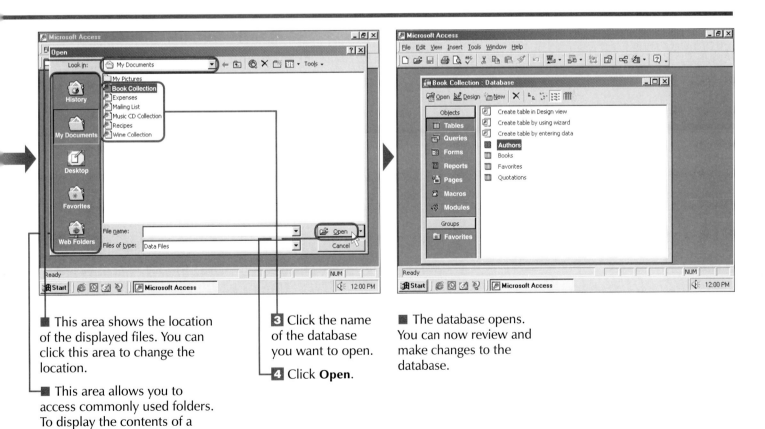

■ This area shows the location of the displayed files. You can click this area to change the location.

■ This area allows you to access commonly used folders. To display the contents of a folder, click the folder.

Note: For information on the commonly used folders, see the top of page 19.

3 Click the name of the database you want to open.

4 Click **Open**.

■ The database opens. You can now review and make changes to the database.

You can use the Database window to open and work with all the objects in your database.

USING THE DATABASE WINDOW

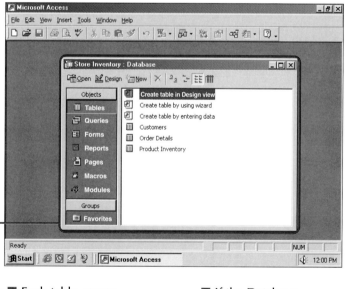

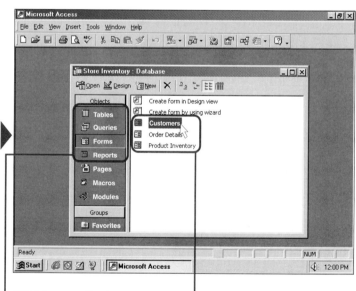

■ Each table, query, form and report in your database appears in the Database window.

■ If the Database window is hidden behind other windows, press the `F11` key to display the window.

■ This area displays the types of objects in your database.

1 Click the type of object you want to work with.

■ This area displays all the objects for the type you selected.

2 Double-click an object to open the object.

What types of objects will I find in the Database window?

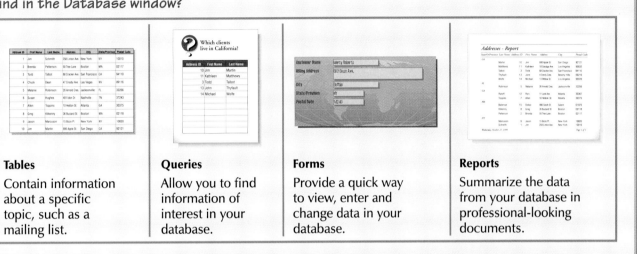

Tables

Contain information about a specific topic, such as a mailing list.

Queries

Allow you to find information of interest in your database.

Forms

Provide a quick way to view, enter and change data in your database.

Reports

Summarize the data from your database in professional-looking documents.

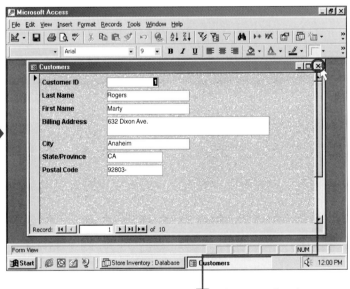

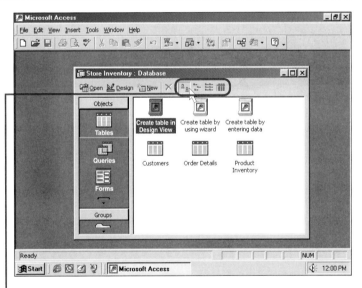

■ Access opens the object and displays its contents on your screen.

3 When you finish working with the object, click ☒ to close the object and return to the Database window.

CHANGE APPEARANCE OF OBJECTS

1 Click one of these buttons to change the appearance of the objects in the Database window.

🔲 Large Icons

🔲 Small Icons

🔲 List

🔲 Details

RENAME A DATABASE OBJECT

You can change the name of a table, query, form or report to better describe the information the object displays.

RENAME A DATABASE OBJECT

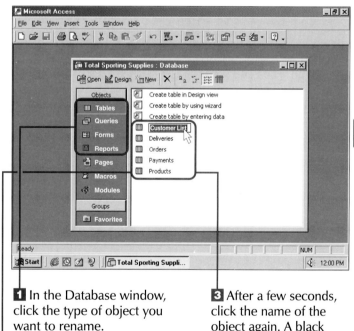

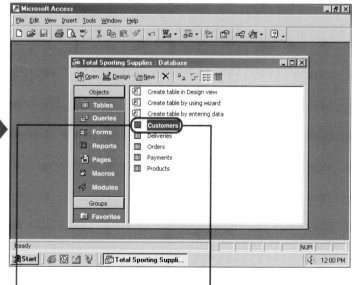

1 In the Database window, click the type of object you want to rename.

2 Click the name of the object you want to rename.

3 After a few seconds, click the name of the object again. A black border appears around the name of the object.

Note: If you accidentally double-click the name of the object, the object will open.

4 Type a new name for the object and then press the Enter key.

■ The object displays the new name.

32

DELETE A DATABASE OBJECT

You can delete a table, query, form or report you no longer need from your database.

Before you delete a table, make sure the table is not used by other objects in your database, such as a form or report.

DELETE A DATABASE OBJECT

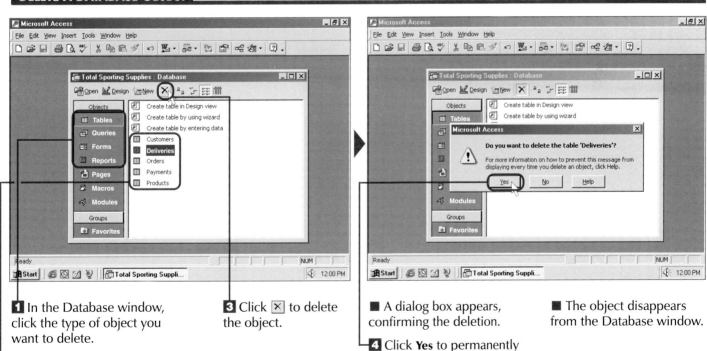

1 In the Database window, click the type of object you want to delete.

2 Click the name of the object you want to delete.

3 Click ⊠ to delete the object.

■ A dialog box appears, confirming the deletion.

4 Click **Yes** to permanently delete the object.

■ The object disappears from the Database window.

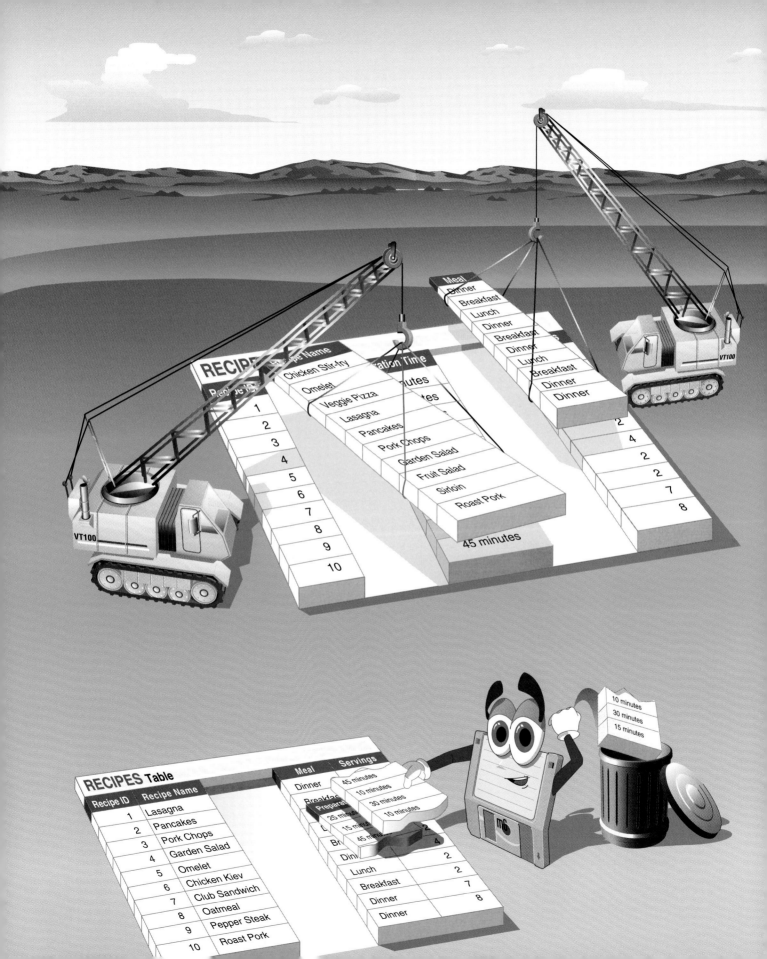

RECIPES Table

Recipe ID	Recipe Name
1	Lasagna
2	Pancakes
3	Pork Chops
4	Garden Salad
5	Omelet
6	Chicken Kiev
7	Club Sandwich
8	Oatmeal
9	Pepper Steak
10	Roast Pork

CHAPTER 3

CREATE TABLES

Are you wondering how to create tables in your database? Learn how in this chapter.

CREATE A TABLE IN THE DATASHEET VIEW

A table stores a collection of information about a specific topic, such as a list of addresses. You can create a table to store new information in your database.

CREATE A TABLE IN THE DATASHEET VIEW

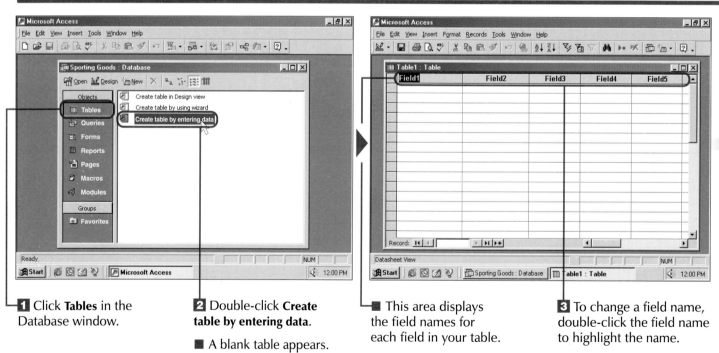

1 Click **Tables** in the Database window.

2 Double-click **Create table by entering data**.

■ A blank table appears.

■ This area displays the field names for each field in your table.

3 To change a field name, double-click the field name to highlight the name.

36

What are the parts of a table?

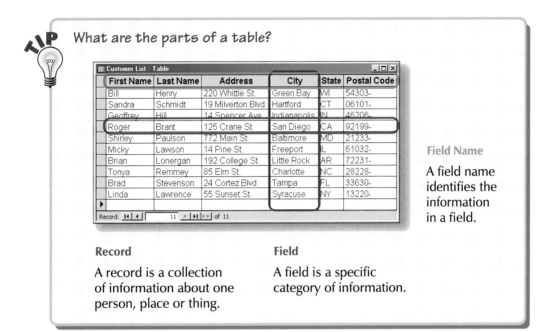

Field Name

A field name identifies the information in a field.

Record

A record is a collection of information about one person, place or thing.

Field

A field is a specific category of information.

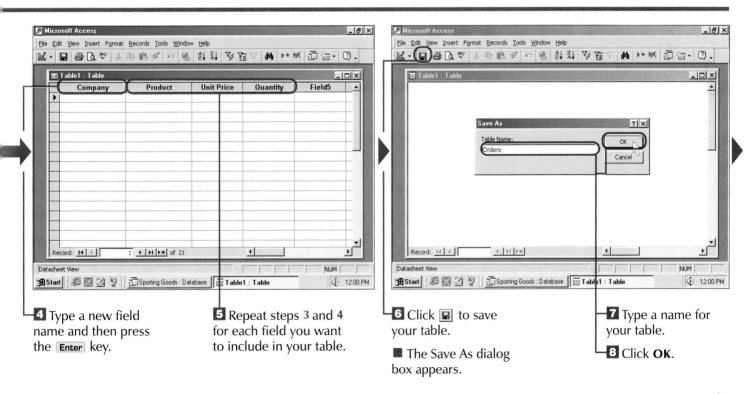

4 Type a new field name and then press the **Enter** key.

5 Repeat steps **3** and **4** for each field you want to include in your table.

6 Click 🖫 to save your table.

■ The Save As dialog box appears.

7 Type a name for your table.

8 Click **OK**.

CONTINUED

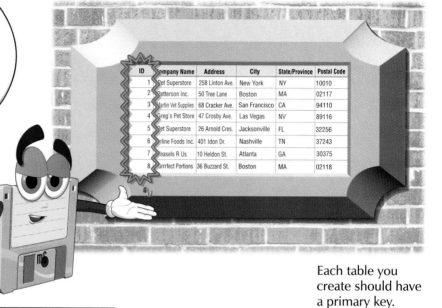

You can have Access create a primary key for your table. A primary key is one or more fields that uniquely identifies each record in a table, such as a field containing ID numbers.

Each table you create should have a primary key.

CREATE A TABLE IN THE DATASHEET VIEW (CONTINUED)

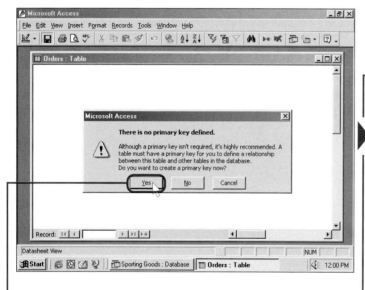

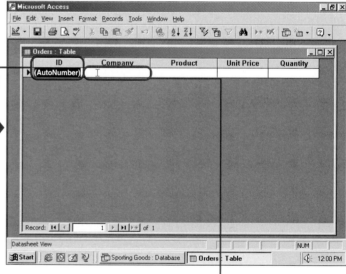

■ A dialog box appears, stating that your table does not have a primary key.

■ 9 To have Access create a primary key for you, click **Yes**.

Note: You can later change the primary key. To change the primary key, see page 102.

■ Access removes the rows and columns that do not contain data.

■ If you selected **Yes** in step **9**, Access adds an ID field to your table to serve as the primary key. This field will automatically display a number for each record you add to your table.

■ 10 To enter the data for a record, click the first empty cell in the row.

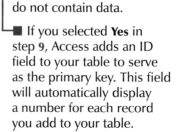

Why do I need to create a primary key in my table?

Access uses the primary key to establish relationships between the tables in your database. Relationships allow Access to bring together related information stored in the tables in your database. For more information on relationships, see page 104.

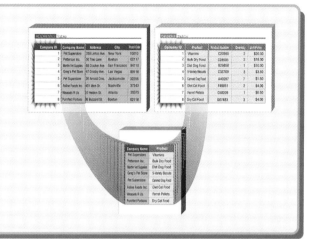

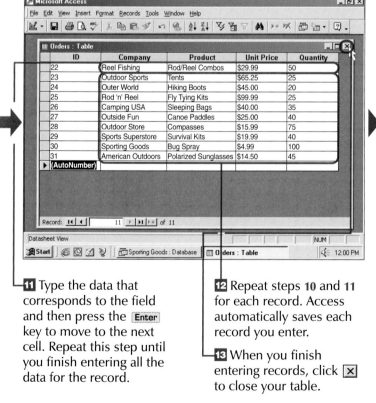

11 Type the data that corresponds to the field and then press the **Enter** key to move to the next cell. Repeat this step until you finish entering all the data for the record.

12 Repeat steps **10** and **11** for each record. Access automatically saves each record you enter.

13 When you finish entering records, click **X** to close your table.

■ The name of your table appears in the Database window.

CREATE A TABLE USING THE TABLE WIZARD

You can use the Table Wizard to help you create a table that suits your needs. The wizard asks you a series of questions and then sets up a table based on your answers.

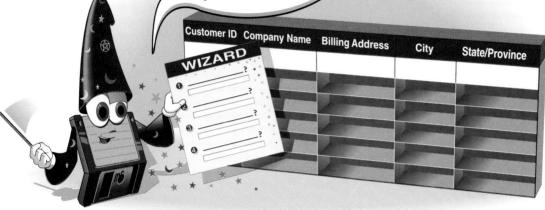

The wizard can help you create a table for business or personal use. The wizard offers tables such as Expenses, Investments, Mailing List, Orders and Recipes.

CREATE A TABLE USING THE TABLE WIZARD

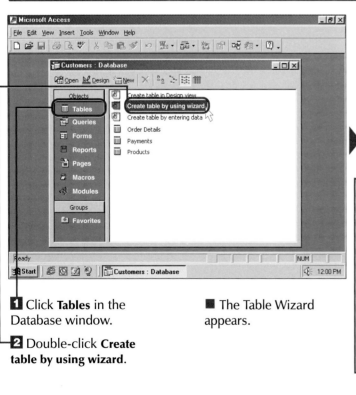

1 Click **Tables** in the Database window.

2 Double-click **Create table by using wizard**.

■ The Table Wizard appears.

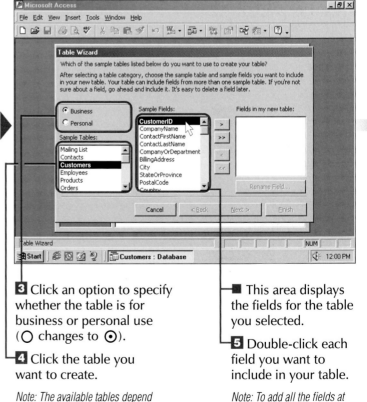

3 Click an option to specify whether the table is for business or personal use (○ changes to ⊙).

4 Click the table you want to create.

Note: The available tables depend on the option you selected in step 3.

■ This area displays the fields for the table you selected.

5 Double-click each field you want to include in your table.

Note: To add all the fields at once, click ⏵⏵ *.*

40

What is a primary key?

A primary key is one or more fields that uniquely identifies each record in a table, such as a field containing ID numbers. When creating a table using the wizard, you can have Access set a primary key for you. Access will create a field that automatically numbers each record in your table. To later change the primary key, see page 102.

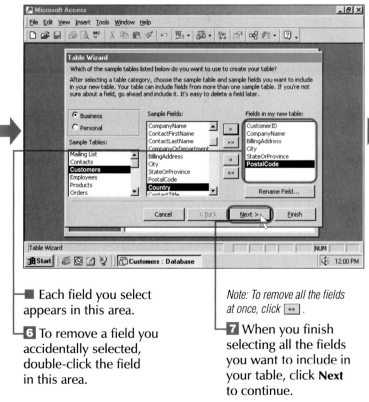

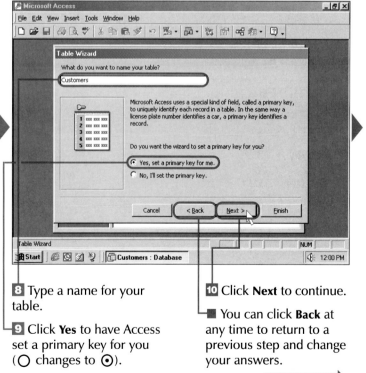

■ Each field you select appears in this area.

■6 To remove a field you accidentally selected, double-click the field in this area.

Note: To remove all the fields at once, click [<<] *.*

■7 When you finish selecting all the fields you want to include in your table, click **Next** to continue.

■8 Type a name for your table.

■9 Click **Yes** to have Access set a primary key for you (○ changes to ⊙).

Note: For information on the primary key, see the top of this page.

■10 Click **Next** to continue.

■ You can click **Back** at any time to return to a previous step and change your answers.

CONTINUED

The Table Wizard shows how your new table relates to the other tables in your database.

Access can bring together information stored in related tables in your database. For more information on relationships, see page 104.

CREATE A TABLE USING THE TABLE WIZARD (CONTINUED)

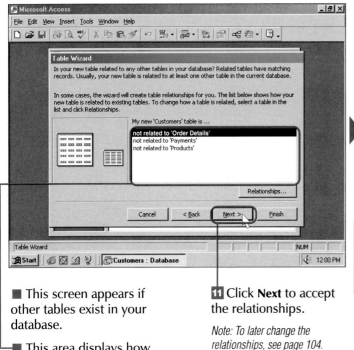

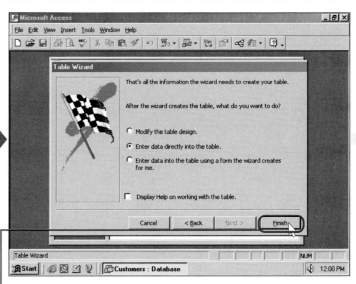

■ This screen appears if other tables exist in your database.

■ This area displays how your new table relates to the other tables in your database.

11 Click **Next** to accept the relationships.

Note: To later change the relationships, see page 104.

12 Click **Finish** to create your table.

Can I rename a field in my table?

Yes. Double-click the name of the field you want to change and then type a new name. For more information on renaming fields, see page 46.

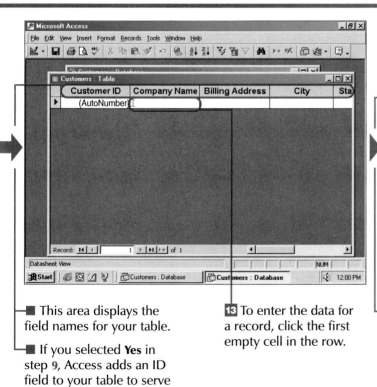

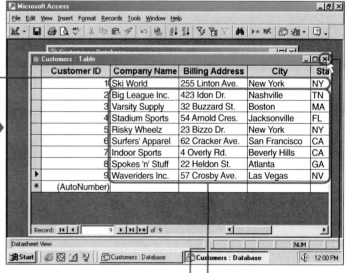

■ This area displays the field names for your table.

■ If you selected **Yes** in step 9, Access adds an ID field to your table to serve as the primary key. This field will automatically display a number for each record you add to the table.

13 To enter the data for a record, click the first empty cell in the row.

14 Type the data that corresponds to the field and then press the `Enter` key to move to the next cell. Repeat this step until you finish entering all the data for the record.

15 Repeat steps 13 and 14 for each record. Access automatically saves each record you enter.

16 When you finish entering records, click ☒ to close your table.

You can open a table to display its contents on your screen. This lets you review and make changes to the table.

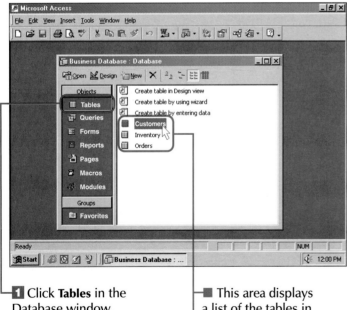

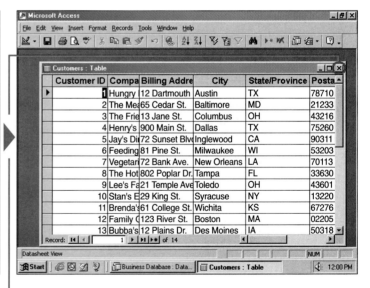

1 Click **Tables** in the Database window.

■ This area displays a list of the tables in your database.

2 Double-click the table you want to open.

■ The table opens. You can now review and make changes to the table.

■ When you finish working with the table, click ☒ to close the table.

■ A dialog box will appear if you did not save changes you made to the layout of the table. Click **Yes** to save the changes.

44

CHANGE COLUMN WIDTH

You can change the width of a column in your table. Increasing the width of a column lets you view data that is too long to display in the column.

Reducing the width of a column allows you to display more fields on your screen at once.

CHANGE COLUMN WIDTH

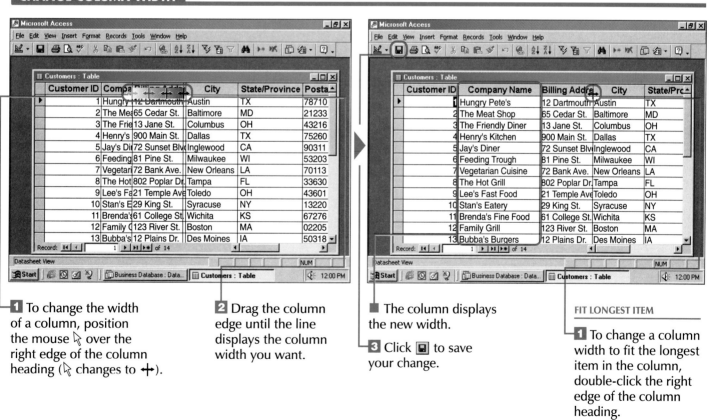

1 To change the width of a column, position the mouse ⌐ over the right edge of the column heading (⌐ changes to ╂).

2 Drag the column edge until the line displays the column width you want.

■ The column displays the new width.

3 Click 🖫 to save your change.

FIT LONGEST ITEM

1 To change a column width to fit the longest item in the column, double-click the right edge of the column heading.

45

RENAME A FIELD

You can give a field a different name to more accurately describe the contents of the field.

RENAME A FIELD

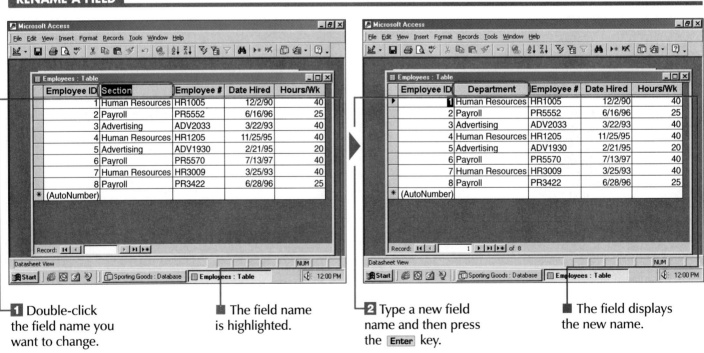

1 Double-click the field name you want to change.

■ The field name is highlighted.

2 Type a new field name and then press the **Enter** key.

■ The field displays the new name.

REARRANGE FIELDS

You can change the order of fields to better organize the information in your table.

Rearranging fields in the Datasheet view will not affect how the fields appear in the Design view or in other objects in the database, such as a form or report. For information on the Datasheet and Design views, see page 71.

REARRANGE FIELDS

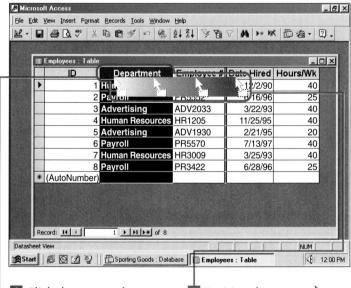

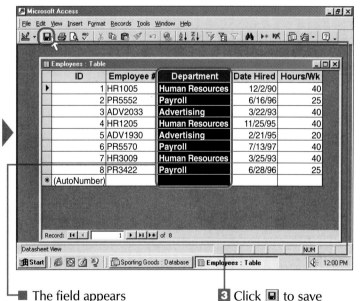

1 Click the name of the field you want to move. The field is highlighted.

2 Position the mouse ⌖ over the field name and then drag the field to a new location.

■ A thick line shows where the field will appear.

■ The field appears in the new location.

3 Click 🖫 to save your change.

You can add a field to your table when you want to include an additional category of information.

A field is a specific category of information in a table. For example, a field can contain the phone numbers of all your clients.

ADD A FIELD

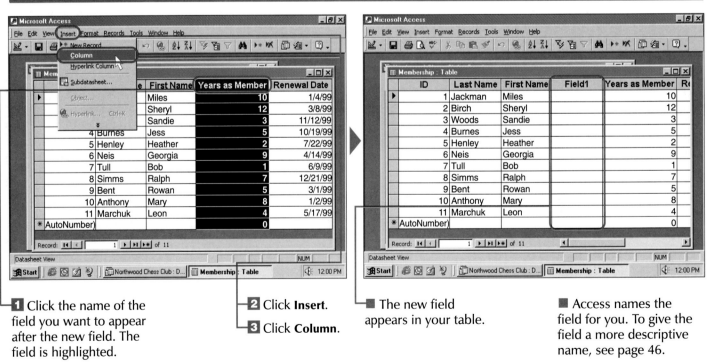

1 Click the name of the field you want to appear after the new field. The field is highlighted.

2 Click **Insert**.

3 Click **Column**.

■ The new field appears in your table.

■ Access names the field for you. To give the field a more descriptive name, see page 46.

DELETE A FIELD

If you no longer need a field, you can permanently delete the field from your table.

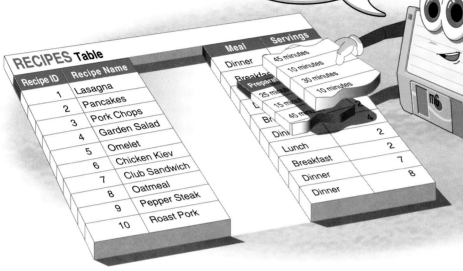

Before you delete a field, make sure the field is not used in other objects in your database, such as a form, query or report.

You cannot delete a field that is part of a relationship. For information on relationships, see page 104.

DELETE A FIELD

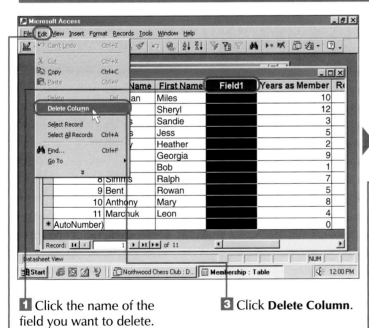

1 Click the name of the field you want to delete. The field is highlighted.

2 Click **Edit**.

3 Click **Delete Column**.

■ A dialog box appears, confirming the deletion.

4 Click **Yes** to permanently delete the field.

■ The field disappears from your table.

CHAPTER 4

EDIT TABLES

Do you want to make changes to your tables? In this chapter you will learn how to edit data, add a new record, hide a field and more.

al Code

010

117

110

16

256

375

118

You can move through the data in your table to review and edit information.

If your table contains a lot of data, your computer screen may not be able to display all the data at once. You can scroll through fields and records to display data that does not appear on your screen.

MOVE THROUGH DATA

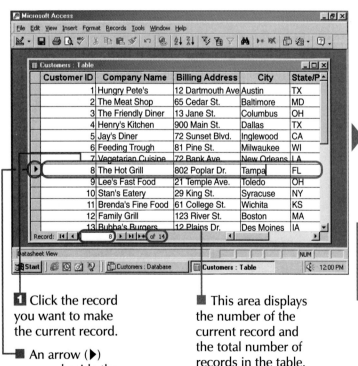

1 Click the record you want to make the current record.

■ An arrow (▶) appears beside the current record.

■ This area displays the number of the current record and the total number of records in the table.

2 To move through the records, click one of the following options.

|◄ First record

◄ Previous record

▶| Next record

▶| Last record

■ To quickly move to a specific record, double-click this area and then type the number of the record you want to display. Then press the **Enter** key.

How do I use my keyboard to move through data in a table?

Press on Keyboard	Description
Page Up	Move up one screen of records
Page Down	Move down one screen of records
Tab	Move to the next field in the current record
↑	Move up one record in the same field
↓	Move down one record in the same field

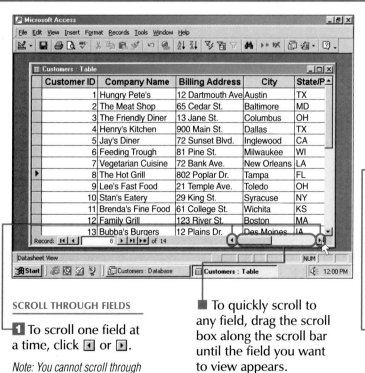

SCROLL THROUGH FIELDS

1 To scroll one field at a time, click ◄ or ►.

Note: You cannot scroll through fields if all the fields appear on your screen.

■ To quickly scroll to any field, drag the scroll box along the scroll bar until the field you want to view appears.

SCROLL THROUGH RECORDS

1 To scroll one record at a time, click ▼ or ▲.

Note: You cannot scroll through records if all the records appear on your screen.

■ To quickly scroll to any record, drag the scroll box along the scroll bar until a yellow box displays the number of the record you want to view.

Before performing many tasks in a table, you must select the data you want to work with. Selected data appears highlighted on your screen.

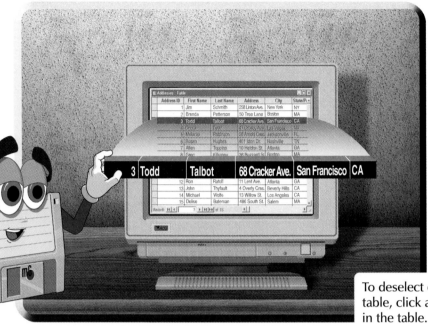

3 | Todd | Talbot | 68 Cracker Ave. | San Francisco | CA

To deselect data in a table, click anywhere in the table.

SELECT DATA

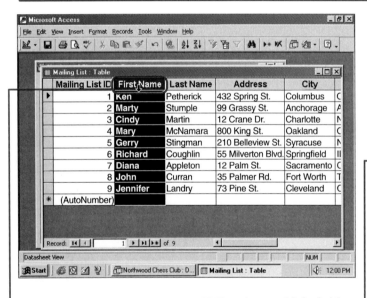

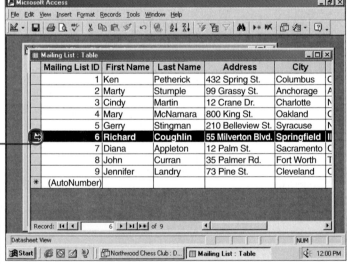

SELECT A FIELD

1 Position the mouse ⌖ over the name of the field you want to select (⌖ changes to ↓) and then click to select the field.

■ To select multiple fields, position the mouse ⌖ over the name of the first field (⌖ changes to ↓). Then drag the mouse ↓ until you highlight all the fields you want to select.

SELECT A RECORD

1 Position the mouse ⌖ over the area to the left of the record you want to select (⌖ changes to →) and then click to select the record.

■ To select multiple records, position the mouse ⌖ over the area to the left of the first record (⌖ changes to →). Then drag the mouse → until you highlight all the records you want to select.

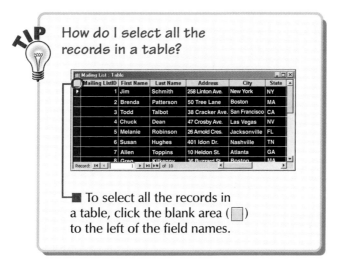

How do I select all the records in a table?

■ To select all the records in a table, click the blank area (□) to the left of the field names.

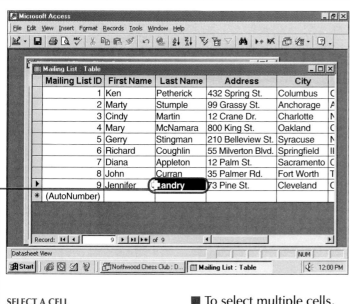

SELECT A CELL

1 Position the mouse I over the left edge of the cell you want to select (I changes to ⇧) and then click to select the cell.

■ To select multiple cells, position the mouse I over the left edge of the first cell (I changes to ⇧). Then drag the mouse ⇧ until you highlight all the cells you want to select.

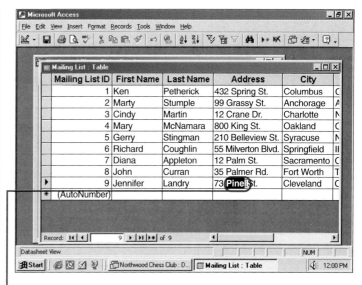

SELECT DATA IN A CELL

1 Position the mouse I over the left edge of the data and then drag the mouse I until you highlight all the data you want to select.

■ To quickly select a word, double-click the word.

You can edit the data in a table to correct a mistake or update the data.

Access automatically saves the changes you make to the data in a table.

EDIT DATA

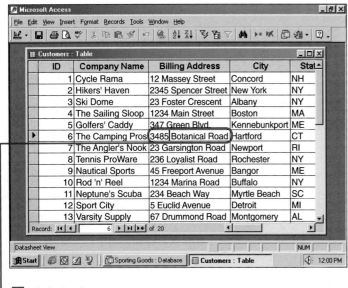

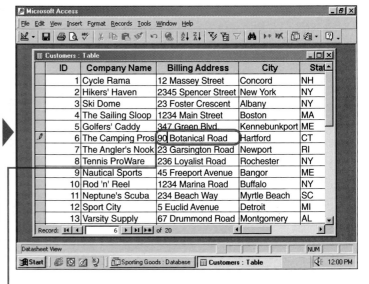

1 Click the location in the cell where you want to edit data.

■ A flashing insertion point appears in the cell.

Note: You can press the ← or → key to move the insertion point to where you want to edit data.

2 To remove the character to the left of the insertion point, press the ◆Backspace key.

3 To insert data where the insertion point flashes on your screen, type the data.

4 When you finish making changes to the data, press the Enter key.

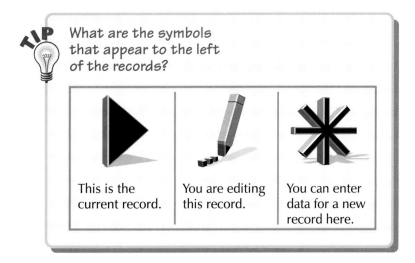

TIP

What are the symbols that appear to the left of the records?

| This is the current record. | You are editing this record. | You can enter data for a new record here. |

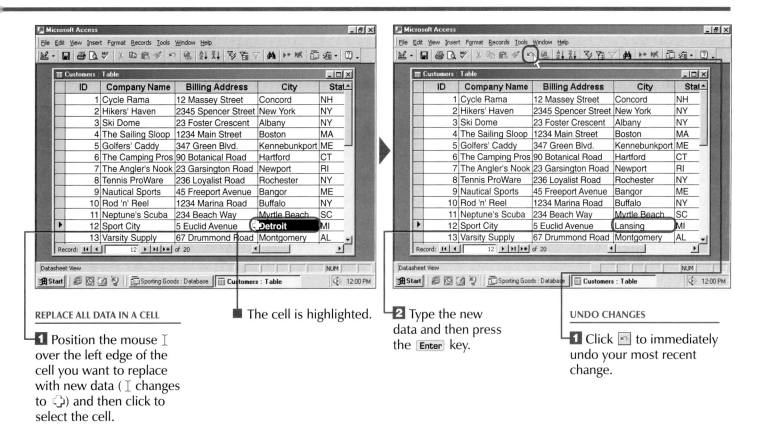

REPLACE ALL DATA IN A CELL

1 Position the mouse I over the left edge of the cell you want to replace with new data (I changes to ⇨) and then click to select the cell.

■ The cell is highlighted.

2 Type the new data and then press the Enter key.

UNDO CHANGES

1 Click to immediately undo your most recent change.

MOVE OR COPY DATA

You can move or copy data to a new location in your table.

MOVE OR COPY DATA

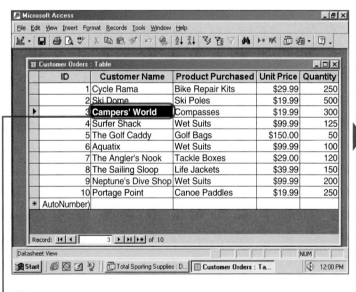

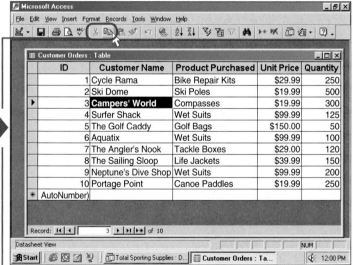

1 To copy data, select the cell(s) containing the data. To select cells, see page 55.

■ To move data, drag the mouse I over the data until you highlight the data.

2 Click one of the following buttons.

✂ Move data

📋 Copy data

Note: The Clipboard toolbar may appear. To hide the Clipboard toolbar, click ⊠ on the toolbar.

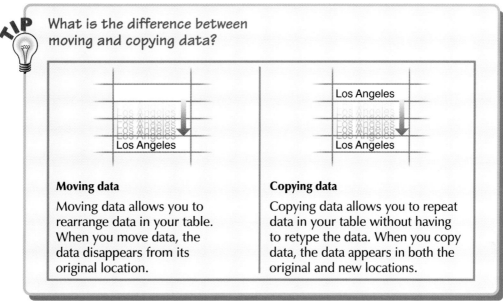

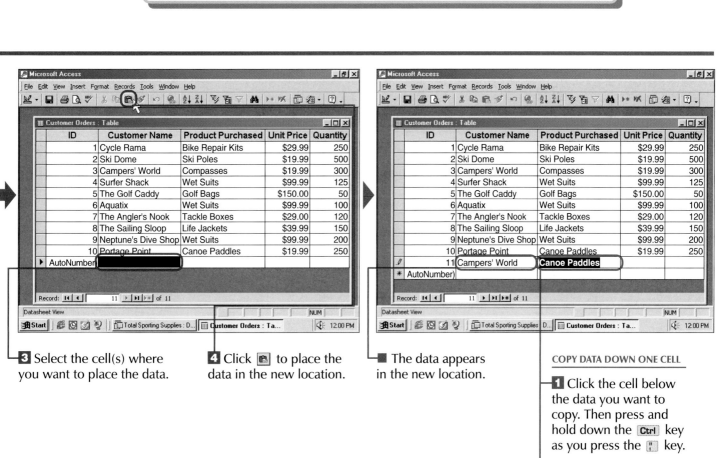

TIP

What is the difference between moving and copying data?

Moving data

Moving data allows you to rearrange data in your table. When you move data, the data disappears from its original location.

Copying data

Copying data allows you to repeat data in your table without having to retype the data. When you copy data, the data appears in both the original and new locations.

3 Select the cell(s) where you want to place the data.

4 Click to place the data in the new location.

■ The data appears in the new location.

COPY DATA DOWN ONE CELL

1 Click the cell below the data you want to copy. Then press and hold down the Ctrl key as you press the key.

■ Access copies the data to the cell.

You can add a record to insert new information into your table. For example, you may want to add information about a new customer.

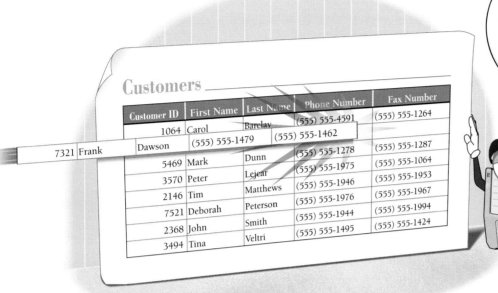

Access automatically saves each new record you add to a table.

ADD A RECORD

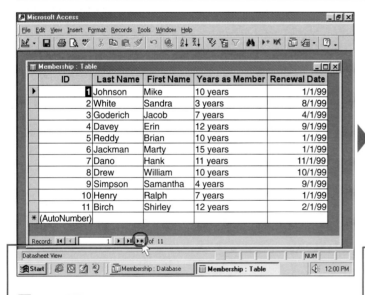

1 Click ▶* to add a new record to your table.

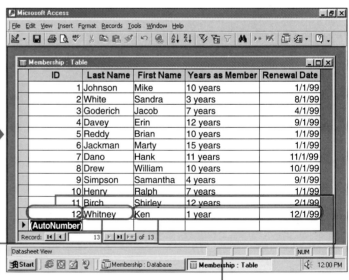

2 Click the first empty cell in the row.

3 Type the data that corresponds to the field and then press the **Enter** key to move to the next cell. Repeat this step until you finish entering all the data for the record.

■ In this example, the ID field automatically displays a number for the new record.

DELETE A RECORD

You can delete a record to permanently remove information you no longer need from a table. For example, you may want to remove information about a product you no longer offer.

Deleting records saves storage space on your computer and reduces clutter in your database.

DELETE A RECORD

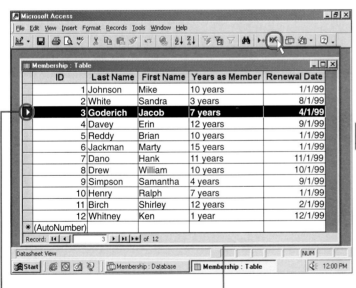

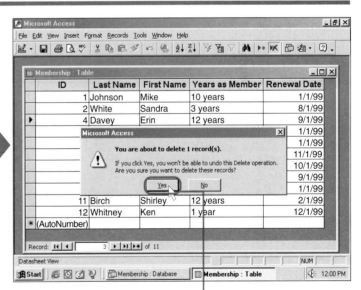

1 Position the mouse ▷ over the area to the left of the record you want to delete (▷ changes to ➡) and then click to select the record.

2 Click ✕ to delete the record.

■ The record disappears.

■ A warning dialog box appears, confirming the deletion.

3 Click **Yes** to permanently delete the record.

You can zoom into any cell in a table to make the contents of the cell easier to review and edit.

Zooming into a cell is useful when a column is not wide enough to display all the data in the cell.

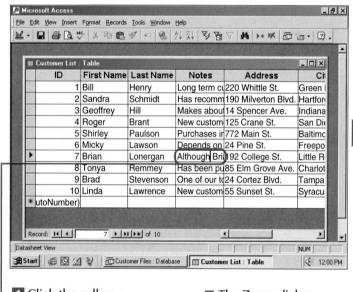

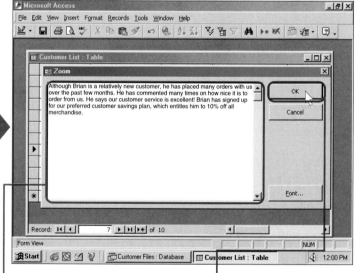

1 Click the cell you want to zoom into.

2 Press and hold down the Shift key as you press the F2 key.

■ The Zoom dialog box appears.

■ This area displays all the data in the cell. You can review and edit the data. To edit data, see page 56.

3 When you finish reviewing and editing the data, click **OK** to close the dialog box.

■ The table will display any changes you made to the data.

DISPLAY A SUBDATASHEET

When viewing the records in a table, you can display a subdatasheet to view and edit related data from another table.

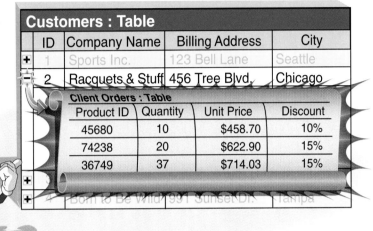

For example, in a table containing customer information, you can display a subdatasheet to view the orders for a customer.

You can only display a subdatasheet when the table you are working with is related to another table. For information on relationships, see page 104.

DISPLAY A SUBDATASHEET

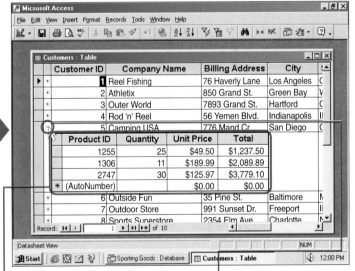

■ When records in a table relate to data in another table, a plus sign (⊞) appears beside each record.

1 Click the plus sign (⊞) beside a record to display the related data from the other table (⊞ changes to ⊟).

■ The related data from the other table appears. You can review and edit the data. To edit data, see page 56.

2 To once again hide the related data, click the minus sign (⊟) beside the record.

You can temporarily hide a field in your table to reduce the amount of information displayed on your screen.

When you hide a field, Access does not delete the field. You can redisplay the field at any time.

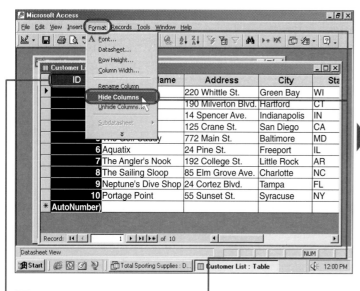

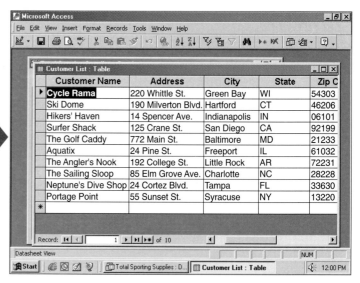

1 Click the name of the field you want to hide. The field is highlighted.

Note: To hide more than one field, select the fields you want to hide. To select multiple fields, see page 54.

2 Click **Format**.

3 Click **Hide Columns**.

■ The field disappears from your table.

When would I hide a field?

Hiding a field can help you review information of interest by removing unnecessary data from your screen. For example, if you want to browse through the names and telephone numbers of your customers, you can hide fields displaying other information.

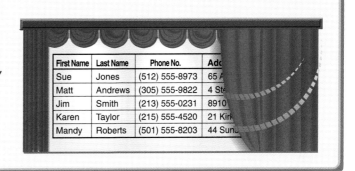

First Name	Last Name	Phone No.	Add
Sue	Jones	(512) 555-8973	65 A
Matt	Andrews	(305) 555-9822	4 St
Jim	Smith	(213) 555-0231	8910
Karen	Taylor	(215) 555-4520	21 Kirk
Mandy	Roberts	(501) 555-8203	44 Sun

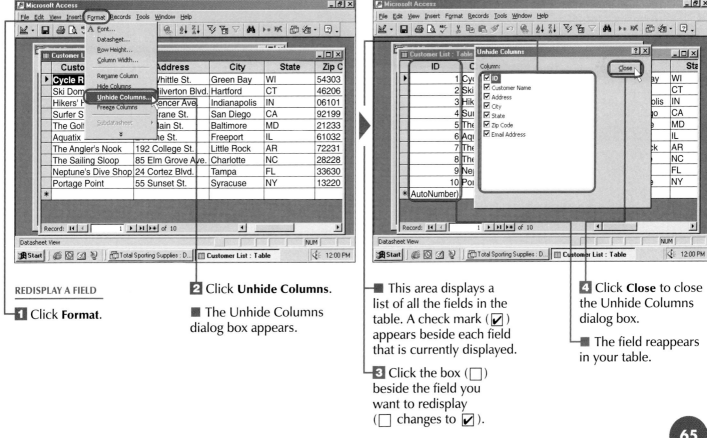

REDISPLAY A FIELD

1 Click **Format**.

2 Click **Unhide Columns**.

■ The Unhide Columns dialog box appears.

■ This area displays a list of all the fields in the table. A check mark (☑) appears beside each field that is currently displayed.

3 Click the box (☐) beside the field you want to redisplay (☐ changes to ☑).

4 Click **Close** to close the Unhide Columns dialog box.

■ The field reappears in your table.

You can freeze a field in your table so the field will remain on your screen at all times.

FREEZE A FIELD

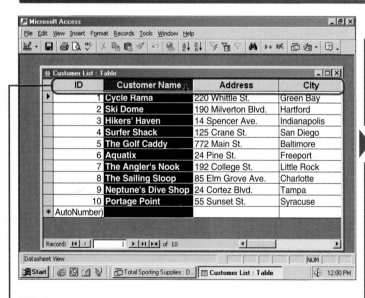

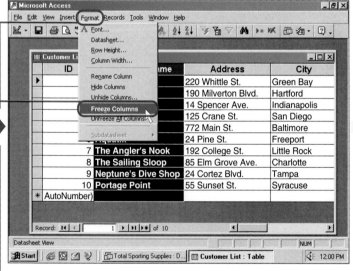

1 Click the name of the field you want to freeze. The field is highlighted.

Note: To freeze more than one field, select the fields you want to freeze. To select multiple fields, see page 54.

2 Click **Format**.

3 Click **Freeze Columns**.

Note: If Freeze Columns does not appear on the menu, position the mouse ⯈ over the bottom of the menu to display all the menu commands.

66

When would I freeze a field?

Freezing a field allows you to keep important data displayed on your screen as you move through data in a large table. For example, you can freeze a field containing product numbers so the numbers will remain on your screen while you scroll through the product information.

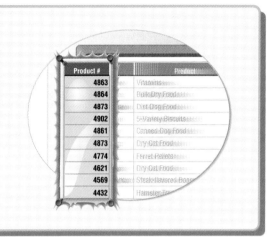

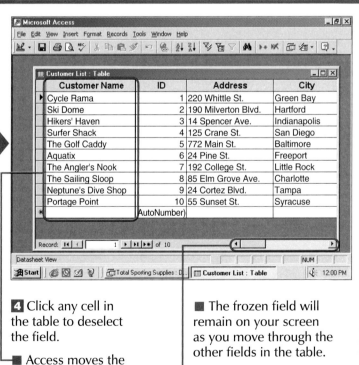

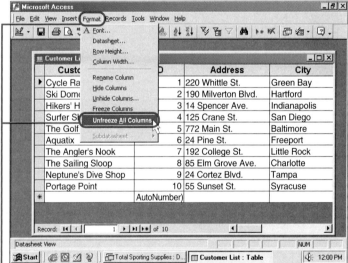

4 Click any cell in the table to deselect the field.

■ Access moves the field to the left side of the table. The vertical line to the right of the field indicates the field is frozen.

■ The frozen field will remain on your screen as you move through the other fields in the table.

■ You can use this scroll bar to move through the fields in the table.

UNFREEZE A FIELD

1 Click **Format**.

2 Click **Unfreeze All Columns**.

Note: If Unfreeze All Columns does not appear on the menu, position the mouse ⌖ over the bottom of the menu to display all the menu commands.

■ When you unfreeze a field, Access does not return the field to its original location in the table. To rearrange fields in a table, see page 47.

CHAPTER 5

DESIGN TABLES

Would you like to customize your tables to better suit your needs? In this chapter you will learn how to specify the type of data a field can contain, set a default value for a field and much more.

CHANGE VIEW OF TABLE

There are two ways you can view a table. Each view allows you to perform different tasks.

CHANGE VIEW OF TABLE

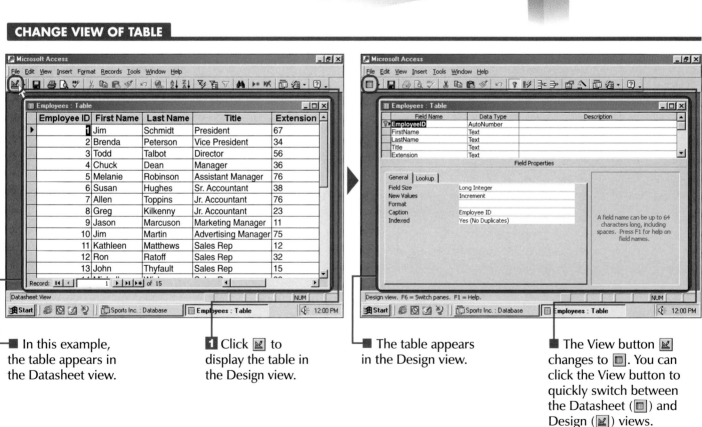

■ In this example, the table appears in the Datasheet view.

1 Click 🖾 to display the table in the Design view.

■ The table appears in the Design view.

■ The View button 🖾 changes to 🔳. You can click the View button to quickly switch between the Datasheet (🔳) and Design (🖾) views.

THE TABLE VIEWS

DATASHEET VIEW

The Datasheet view displays all the records in a table. You can enter, edit and review records in this view.

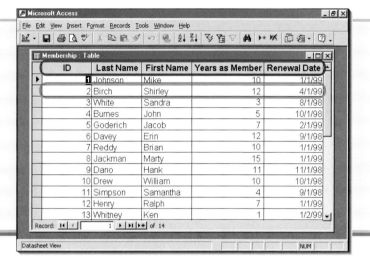

Field Name

A field name identifies the information within a field.

Record

A record is a collection of information about one person, place or thing.

DESIGN VIEW

The Design view allows you to change the structure of a table. You can change the settings in this view to specify the kind of information you can enter in a table.

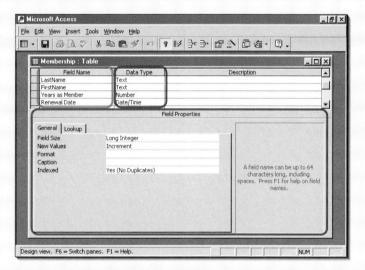

Field Name

A field name identifies the information within a field.

Data Type

The data type determines the type of information you can enter in a field, such as text, numbers or dates. For example, you cannot enter text in a field with the Number data type.

Field Properties

The field properties are a set of characteristics that provide additional control over the information you can enter in a field. For example, you can specify the maximum number of characters a field will accept.

You can display the properties for each field in your table. The field properties are a set of characteristics that control the information you can enter in a field.

For example, a field property can specify the maximum number of characters a field will accept.

DISPLAY FIELD PROPERTIES

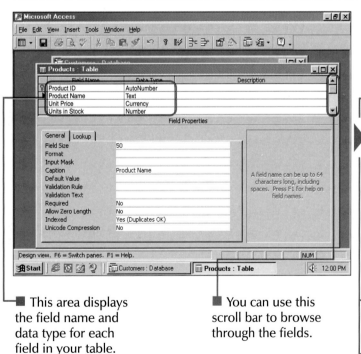

■ This area displays the field name and data type for each field in your table.

■ You can use this scroll bar to browse through the fields.

■ Click the name of a field to display the properties for the field.

■ A triangle (▶) appears beside the field name.

■ This area displays the properties for the field. The available properties depend on the data type of the field.

ADD A FIELD DESCRIPTION

You can add a description to a field to help you determine the kind of information you should enter in the field.

ADD A FIELD DESCRIPTION

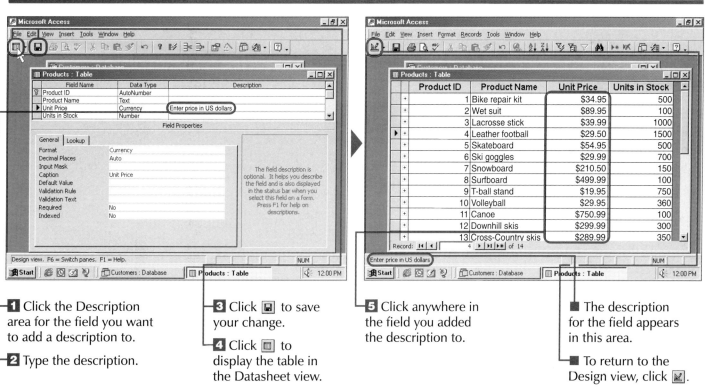

1 Click the Description area for the field you want to add a description to.

2 Type the description.

3 Click 🖫 to save your change.

4 Click 🖩 to display the table in the Datasheet view.

5 Click anywhere in the field you added the description to.

■ The description for the field appears in this area.

■ To return to the Design view, click 🖳.

CHANGE A DATA TYPE

You can change the type of data you can enter in a field.

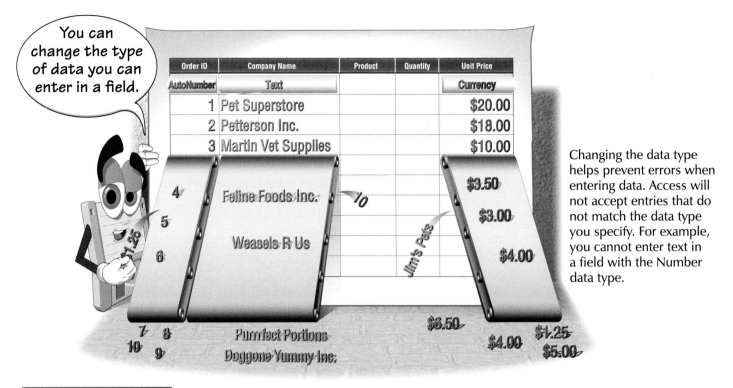

Changing the data type helps prevent errors when entering data. Access will not accept entries that do not match the data type you specify. For example, you cannot enter text in a field with the Number data type.

CHANGE A DATA TYPE

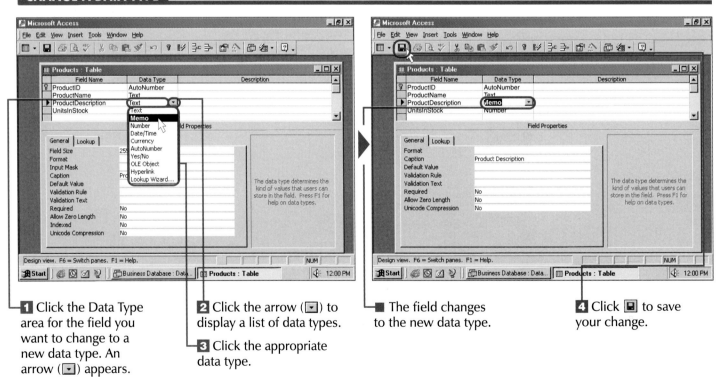

1 Click the Data Type area for the field you want to change to a new data type. An arrow (▼) appears.

2 Click the arrow (▼) to display a list of data types.

3 Click the appropriate data type.

■ The field changes to the new data type.

4 Click 🖫 to save your change.

DATA TYPES

Text

Accepts entries up to 255 characters long that include any combination of text and numbers, such as a name or address. Make sure you use this data type for numbers you will not use in calculations, such as phone numbers and zip codes.

AutoNumber

Automatically numbers each record for you.

Memo

Accepts entries up to 65,535 characters long that include any combination of text and numbers, such as notes, comments and lengthy descriptions.

Yes/No

Accepts only one of two values–Yes/No, True/False or On/Off.

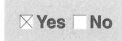

Number

Accepts numbers you want to use in calculations.

OLE Object

Accepts OLE objects. An OLE object is an object created in another program, such as a document, spreadsheet or picture.

Date/Time

Accepts only dates and times.

Hyperlink

Accepts hyperlinks you can select to jump to a document or Web page.

Currency

Accepts only monetary values.

Lookup Wizard

Starts the Lookup Wizard so you can create a list of items to choose from when entering data in a field. For more information on the Lookup Wizard, see page 92.

You can select a format to customize the way information appears in a field. For example, you can select the way you want dates to appear.

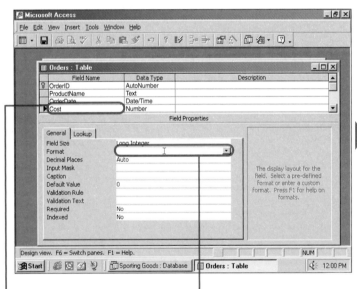

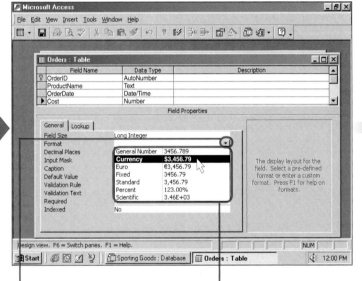

1 Click the field that contains the data you want to display in a new format.

2 Click the area beside **Format**. An arrow (▼) appears.

3 Click the arrow (▼) to display a list of formats. A list only appears for fields with the Number, Date/Time, Currency, AutoNumber or Yes/No data type. For information on data types, see page 75.

Note: For information on some of the available formats, see the top of page 77.

4 Click the format you want to use.

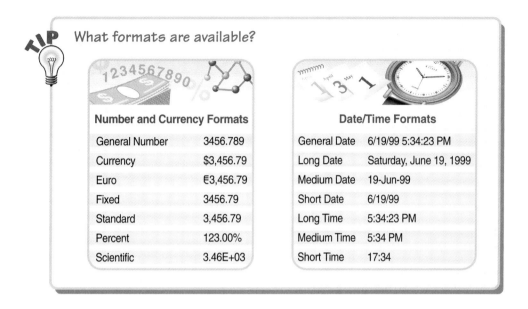

What formats are available?

Number and Currency Formats	
General Number	3456.789
Currency	$3,456.79
Euro	€3,456.79
Fixed	3456.79
Standard	3,456.79
Percent	123.00%
Scientific	3.46E+03

Date/Time Formats	
General Date	6/19/99 5:34:23 PM
Long Date	Saturday, June 19, 1999
Medium Date	19-Jun-99
Short Date	6/19/99
Long Time	5:34:23 PM
Medium Time	5:34 PM
Short Time	17:34

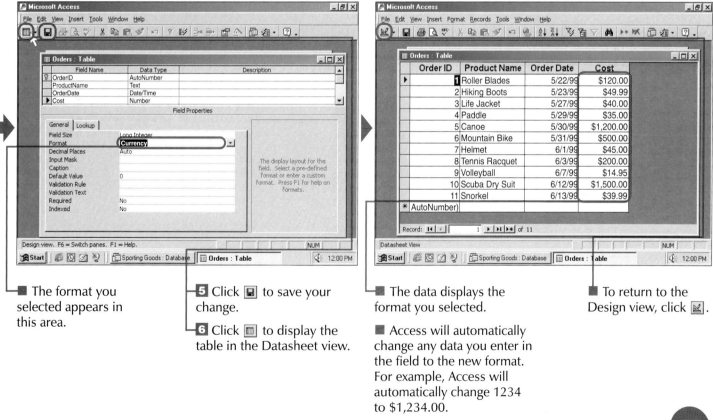

■ The format you selected appears in this area.

5 Click 🖫 to save your change.

6 Click 🖩 to display the table in the Datasheet view.

■ The data displays the format you selected.

■ Access will automatically change any data you enter in the field to the new format. For example, Access will automatically change 1234 to $1,234.00.

■ To return to the Design view, click 🖳.

CHANGE THE FIELD SIZE

You can reduce errors by changing the size of a text or number field. Access can process smaller field sizes more quickly.

You can change the size of a text field to specify the maximum number of characters the field will accept. You can change the size of a number field to specify the type of number the field will accept.

For example, if you set the size of a text field to 2, you can enter CA but not California.

First Name	Last Name	City
Jim	Schmith	New York
Brenda	Petterson	Boston
Jim	Martin	San Diego
Melanie	Robinson	Jacksonville
Susan	Hughes	Nashville
Allen	Toppins	Atlanta

State

N Y
M A
C A
F L
T N
G A

TEXT FIELDS

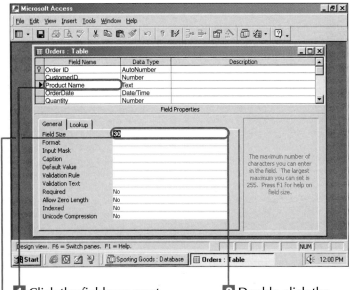

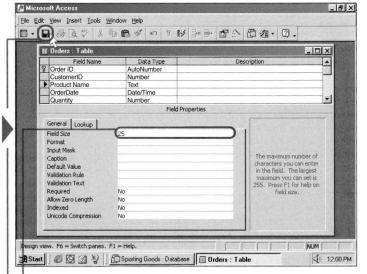

1 Click the field you want to accept a maximum number of characters.

■ The area beside **Field Size** displays the maximum number of characters you can currently type in the field.

2 Double-click the number to highlight the number.

3 Type the maximum number of characters you want the field to accept. You can enter a number from 1 to 255.

4 Click 🖫 to save your change.

■ A warning dialog box appears if you reduce the size of a field that contains data. Access will shorten data that is longer than the new field size. To continue, click **Yes**.

78

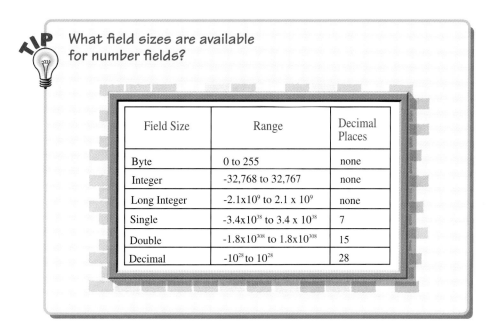

TIP

What field sizes are available
for number fields?

Field Size	Range	Decimal Places
Byte	0 to 255	none
Integer	-32,768 to 32,767	none
Long Integer	-2.1×10^9 to 2.1×10^9	none
Single	-3.4×10^{38} to 3.4×10^{38}	7
Double	-1.8×10^{308} to 1.8×10^{308}	15
Decimal	-10^{28} to 10^{28}	28

NUMBER FIELDS

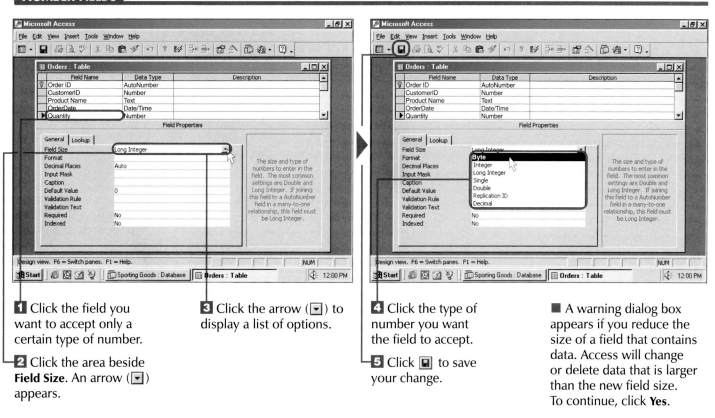

1 Click the field you want to accept only a certain type of number.

2 Click the area beside **Field Size**. An arrow (▾) appears.

3 Click the arrow (▾) to display a list of options.

4 Click the type of number you want the field to accept.

5 Click 🖫 to save your change.

■ A warning dialog box appears if you reduce the size of a field that contains data. Access will change or delete data that is larger than the new field size. To continue, click **Yes**.

You can specify how many decimal places you want numbers in a field to display.

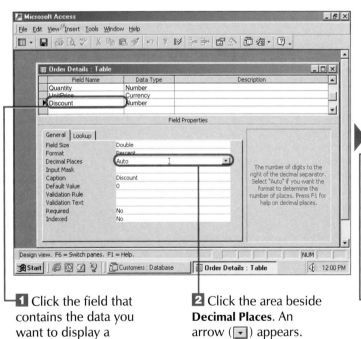

1 Click the field that contains the data you want to display a specific number of decimal places.

2 Click the area beside **Decimal Places**. An arrow (▼) appears.

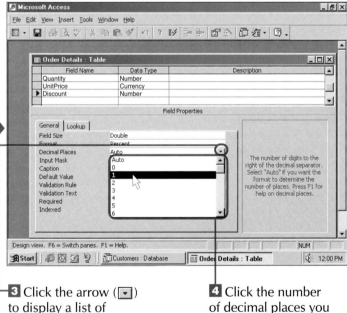

3 Click the arrow (▼) to display a list of decimal place options.

4 Click the number of decimal places you want the data in the field to display.

Why doesn't my data display the number of decimal places I specified?

Changing the number of decimal places will not change the appearance of data if the Format property of the field is blank or set to General Number. To change the Format property of a field, see page 76.

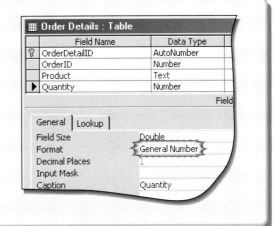

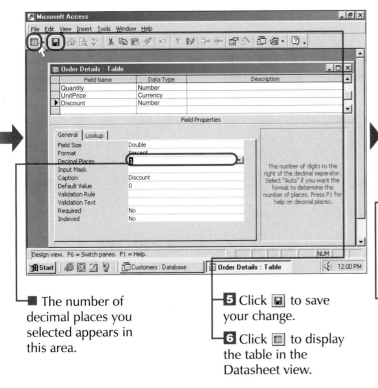

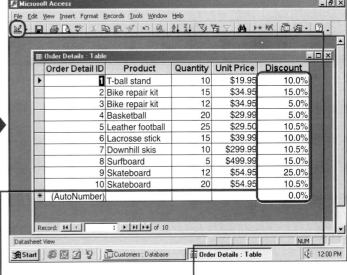

■ The number of decimal places you selected appears in this area.

5 Click 🖫 to save your change.

6 Click 🔲 to display the table in the Datasheet view.

■ The data displays the number of decimal places you specified.

■ Access will automatically display any data you enter in the field with the correct number of decimal places.

Note: If Access changes decimal places you type to zeros (example: 12.34 changes to 12.00), you need to change the field size. To change the field size, see page 78.

■ To return to the Design view, click 🖾.

SET A DEFAULT VALUE

You can specify a value that you want to appear automatically in a field each time you add a new record. This saves you from having to repeatedly type the same data.

For example, if most of your customers live in California, you can set "California" as the default value for the State field.

SET A DEFAULT VALUE

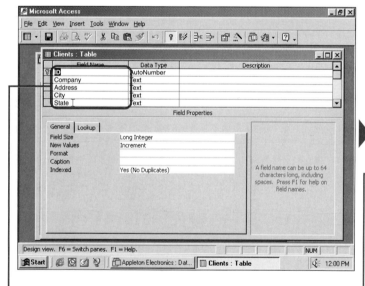

1 Click the field you want to have a default value.

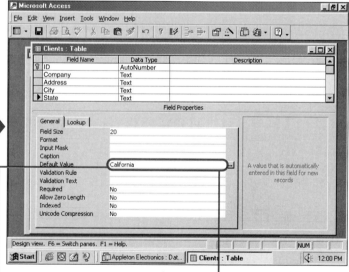

2 Click the area beside **Default Value**.

3 Type the text or number you want to set as the default value.

Can I set the current date as the default value for a field?

You can have Access automatically add the current date to a field each time you add a new record. This is useful for fields containing invoice or shipping dates. Perform the steps below, typing **=Date()** in step 3.

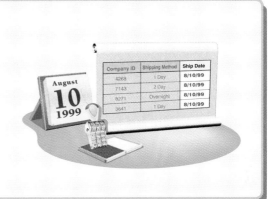

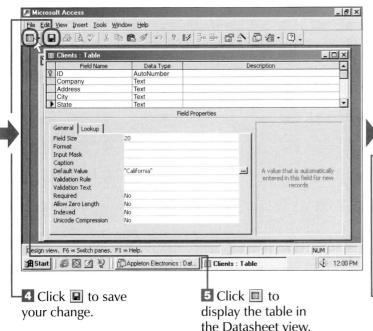

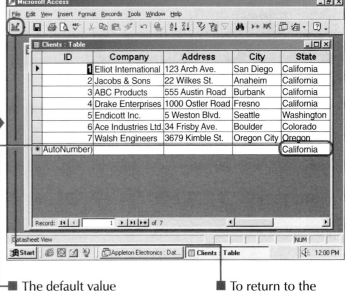

4 Click 🖫 to save your change.

5 Click 🏢 to display the table in the Datasheet view.

■ The default value automatically appears in the field each time you add a new record. You can accept the value or type another value.

■ To return to the Design view, click 🔙.

DATA ENTRY REQUIRED

> You can specify that a field must contain data for each record. This prevents you from leaving out important information when entering data.

	Qty	Amount	Invoice #
Tennis Balls	505	$3.00	**16437**
Golf Clubs	736	$550.95	**16438**
Biking Shorts	377	$34.99	**16439**
Running Shoes	638	$99.49	**16440**
Hats	894	$15.99	**16441**

For example, a table containing invoice information can require data in the Invoice Number field.

DATA ENTRY REQUIRED

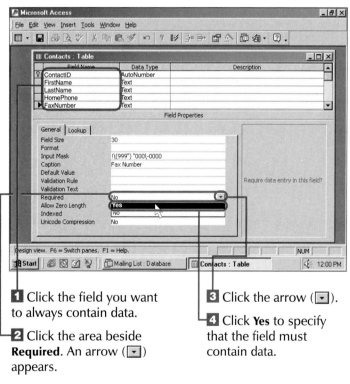

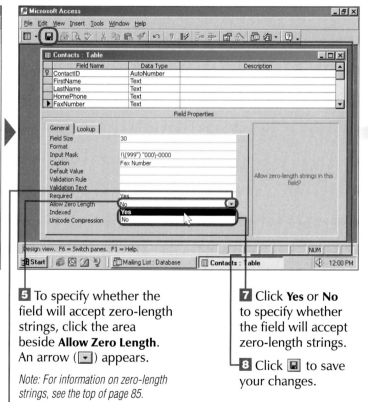

1 Click the field you want to always contain data.

2 Click the area beside **Required**. An arrow (▼) appears.

3 Click the arrow (▼).

4 Click **Yes** to specify that the field must contain data.

5 To specify whether the field will accept zero-length strings, click the area beside **Allow Zero Length**. An arrow (▼) appears.

Note: For information on zero-length strings, see the top of page 85.

6 Click the arrow (▼).

7 Click **Yes** or **No** to specify whether the field will accept zero-length strings.

8 Click 🖫 to save your changes.

What is a zero-length string?

A zero-length string is an entry that contains no characters. A zero-length string is useful if you must enter data in a field, but no data exists. For example, if the Fax Number field must contain data, but a customer does not have a fax machine, you can enter a zero-length string in the field.

To enter a zero-length string, type "" in the cell. The cell will appear empty.

ID	First Name	Last Name	Phone	Fax
1	Theresa	Garcia	555-4433	555-4434
2	Daniel	Goodland	555-1234	
3	Susan	Hughes	555-6677	555-6678
4	Greg	Kilkenny	555-1215	555-1216
5	Stephen	MacDonald	555-2200	
6	Jim	Smith	555-1543	555-1550
7	Allen	Toppins	555-6235	555-6236
8	Linda	Vieira	555-8976	

CAN CONTAIN ZERO-LENGTH STRINGS

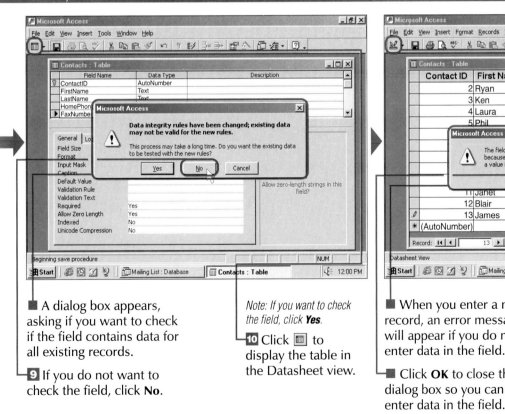

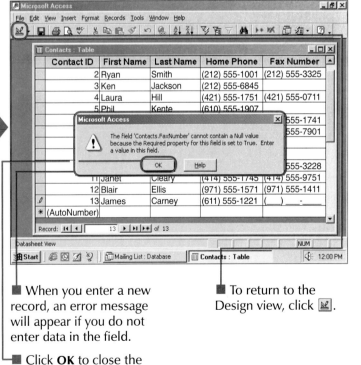

■ A dialog box appears, asking if you want to check if the field contains data for all existing records.

9 If you do not want to check the field, click **No**.

*Note: If you want to check the field, click **Yes**.*

10 Click 🔲 to display the table in the Datasheet view.

■ When you enter a new record, an error message will appear if you do not enter data in the field.

■ Click **OK** to close the dialog box so you can enter data in the field.

■ To return to the Design view, click 🔲.

ADD A VALIDATION RULE

You can add a validation rule to a field to help reduce errors when entering data. A field that uses a validation rule can only accept data that meets the requirements you specify.

ADD A VALIDATION RULE

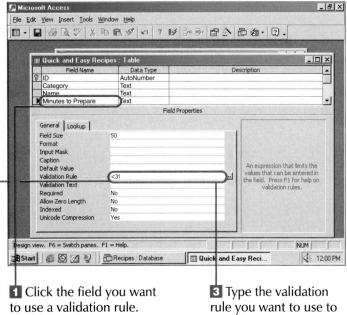

1 Click the field you want to use a validation rule.

2 Click the area beside **Validation Rule**.

3 Type the validation rule you want to use to limit the data you can enter into the field.

Note: For examples of validation rules, see the top of page 87.

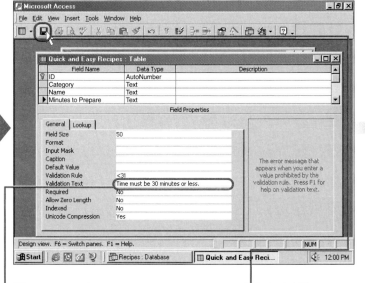

4 To create the error message you want to appear when you enter incorrect data, click the area beside **Validation Text**.

5 Type the error message you want to appear.

6 Click 🖫 to save your changes.

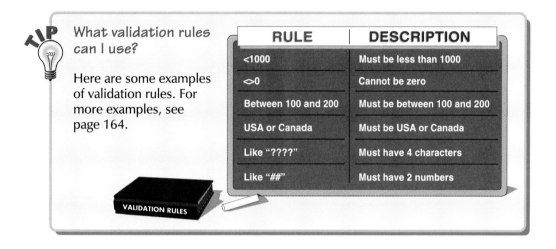

TIP

What validation rules can I use?

Here are some examples of validation rules. For more examples, see page 164.

RULE	DESCRIPTION
<1000	Must be less than 1000
<>0	Cannot be zero
Between 100 and 200	Must be between 100 and 200
USA or Canada	Must be USA or Canada
Like "????"	Must have 4 characters
Like "##"	Must have 2 numbers

VALIDATION RULES

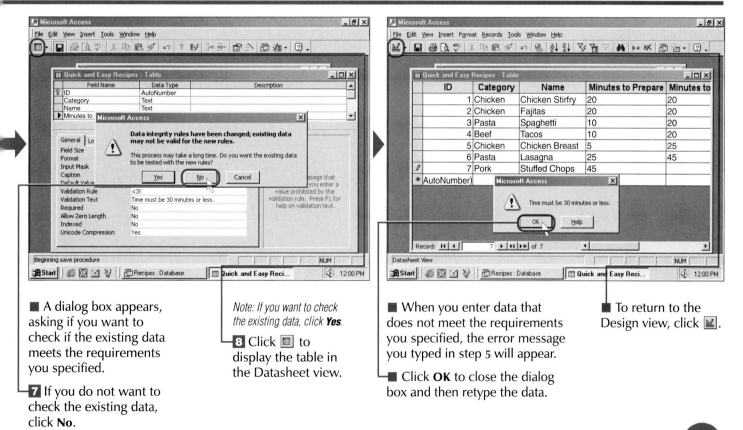

■ A dialog box appears, asking if you want to check if the existing data meets the requirements you specified.

7 If you do not want to check the existing data, click **No**.

*Note: If you want to check the existing data, click **Yes**.*

8 Click ▦ to display the table in the Datasheet view.

■ When you enter data that does not meet the requirements you specified, the error message you typed in step **5** will appear.

■ Click **OK** to close the dialog box and then retype the data.

■ To return to the Design view, click ▨.

For example, you can create a Yes/No field to specify whether each student passed a course.

CREATE A YES/NO FIELD

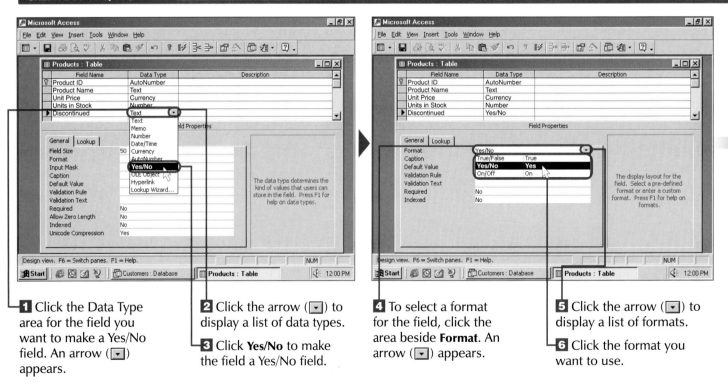

1 Click the Data Type area for the field you want to make a Yes/No field. An arrow (▼) appears.

2 Click the arrow (▼) to display a list of data types.

3 Click **Yes/No** to make the field a Yes/No field.

4 To select a format for the field, click the area beside **Format**. An arrow (▼) appears.

5 Click the arrow (▼) to display a list of formats.

6 Click the format you want to use.

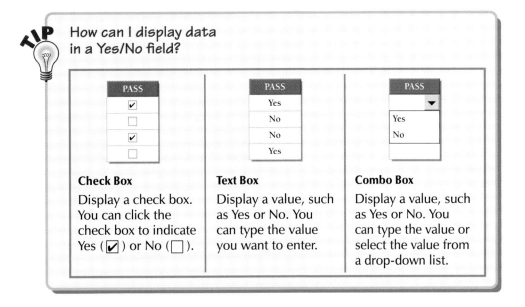

TIP

How can I display data in a Yes/No field?

Check Box

Display a check box. You can click the check box to indicate Yes (☑) or No (☐).

Text Box

Display a value, such as Yes or No. You can type the value you want to enter.

Combo Box

Display a value, such as Yes or No. You can type the value or select the value from a drop-down list.

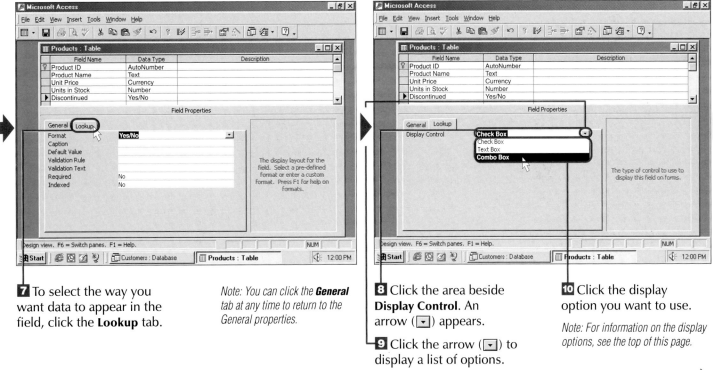

7 To select the way you want data to appear in the field, click the **Lookup** tab.

*Note: You can click the **General** tab at any time to return to the General properties.*

8 Click the area beside **Display Control**. An arrow (▾) appears.

9 Click the arrow (▾) to display a list of options.

10 Click the display option you want to use.

Note: For information on the display options, see the top of this page.

CONTINUED

CREATE A YES/NO FIELD

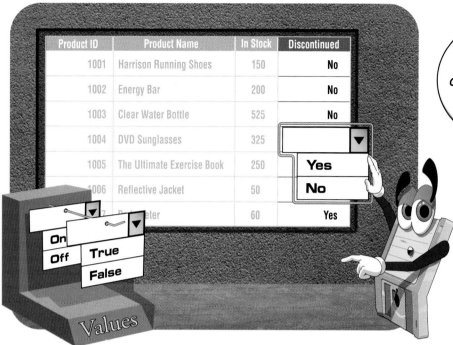

When creating a Yes/No field that uses a Combo Box, you can specify the values you want to appear in the drop-down list for the field.

Product ID	Product Name	In Stock	Discontinued
1001	Harrison Running Shoes	150	No
1002	Energy Bar	200	No
1003	Clear Water Bottle	525	No
1004	DVD Sunglasses	325	
1005	The Ultimate Exercise Book	250	
1006	Reflective Jacket	50	
	eter	60	Yes

CREATE A YES/NO FIELD (CONTINUED)

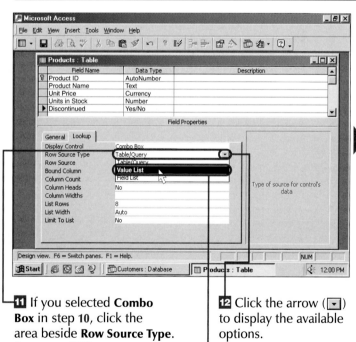

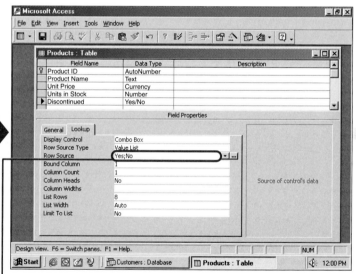

11 If you selected **Combo Box** in step **10**, click the area beside **Row Source Type**. An arrow (▼) appears.

*Note: If you selected **Check Box** or **Text Box** in step 10, skip to step 16.*

12 Click the arrow (▼) to display the available options.

13 Click **Value List** to type the values you want to appear in the drop-down list for the field.

14 Click the area beside **Row Source**.

15 Type the two values you want to appear in the drop-down list for the field. Separate the values with a semicolon (;).

Note: The values you type should match the format you selected in step 6.

90

How can I speed up entering data in a Yes/No field?

When you add a record to your table, Access automatically displays the **No** value in a Yes/No field. If most of your records require a **Yes** value, you can change the default value to **Yes**. To set the default value for a field, see page 82.

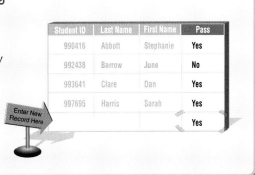

Student ID	Last Name	First Name	Pass
990416	Abbott	Stephanie	Yes
992438	Barrow	June	No
993641	Clare	Dan	Yes
997695	Harris	Sarah	Yes
			Yes

Enter New Record Here

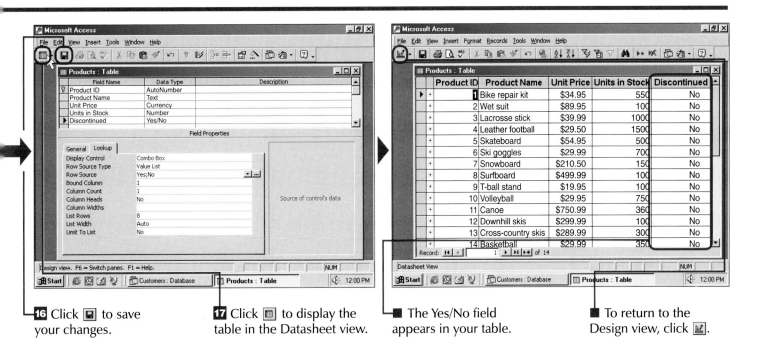

16 Click 🖬 to save your changes.

17 Click 🖩 to display the table in the Datasheet view.

■ The Yes/No field appears in your table.

■ To return to the Design view, click 🖾.

CREATE A LOOKUP COLUMN

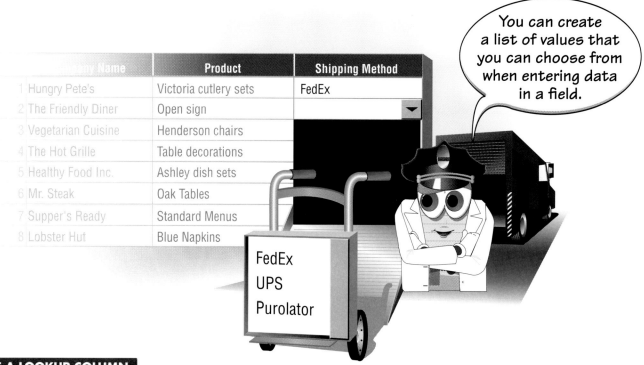

You can create a list of values that you can choose from when entering data in a field.

Company Name	Product	Shipping Method
1 Hungry Pete's	Victoria cutlery sets	FedEx
2 The Friendly Diner	Open sign	
3 Vegetarian Cuisine	Henderson chairs	
4 The Hot Grille	Table decorations	
5 Healthy Food Inc.	Ashley dish sets	
6 Mr. Steak	Oak Tables	
7 Supper's Ready	Standard Menus	
8 Lobster Hut	Blue Napkins	

FedEx
UPS
Purolator

CREATE A LOOKUP COLUMN

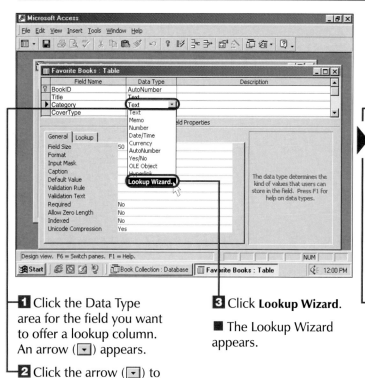

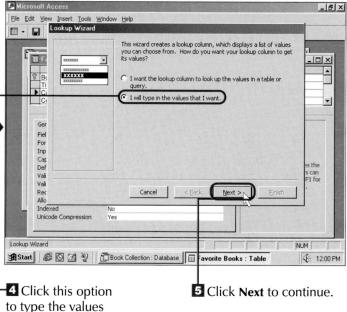

1 Click the Data Type area for the field you want to offer a lookup column. An arrow (▾) appears.

2 Click the arrow (▾) to display a list of data types.

3 Click **Lookup Wizard**.

■ The Lookup Wizard appears.

4 Click this option to type the values you want the lookup column to offer (○ changes to ⊙).

5 Click **Next** to continue.

TIP

Why would I create a lookup column?

Creating a lookup column is useful if you repeatedly enter the same data in a field. For example, if your customers reside in three states, you can create a lookup column that displays the three states, such as CA, TX and IL.

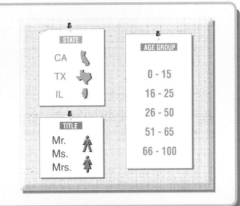

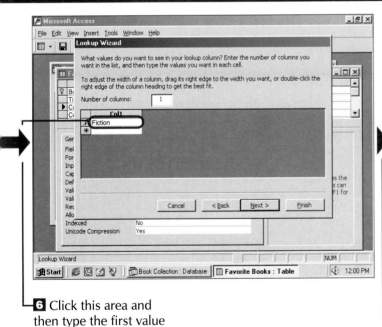

6 Click this area and then type the first value you want to appear in the lookup column.

7 To enter the next value, press the **Tab** key and then type the value.

8 Repeat step **7** for each value you want to appear in the lookup column.

9 Click **Next** to continue.

CONTINUED

CREATE A LOOKUP COLUMN

When entering data in a field, you can select a value from a lookup column to save time and reduce errors.

Order ID	Company Name	Product	Qty	Ship
1	Hungry Pete's	Victoria cutlery sets	3	Ground
2	The Friendly Diner	Open sign	2	1 Day Air
3	Vegetarian Cuisine	Henderson chairs	4	4 Day Air
4	The Hot Grille	Table decorations	20	4 Day Air
5	Healthy Foods	Ashley dish sets		
6	Mr. Steak	Oak tables		
7	Supper's Ready	Standard Menus		

1 Day Air ▼
Ground
1 Day Air
2 Day Air
4 Day Air

CREATE A LOOKUP COLUMN (CONTINUED)

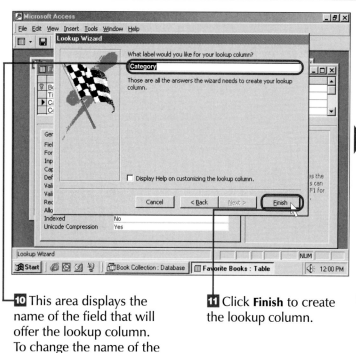

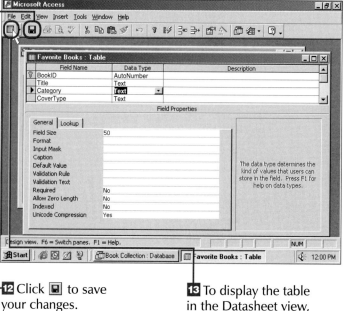

■10 This area displays the name of the field that will offer the lookup column. To change the name of the field, type a new name.

■11 Click **Finish** to create the lookup column.

■12 Click 🖫 to save your changes.

■13 To display the table in the Datasheet view, click 🔲.

94

Do I have to select a value from a lookup column?

No. If a lookup column does not display the value you want to use, you can type a different value. To hide a lookup column you displayed without selecting a value, click outside the lookup column.

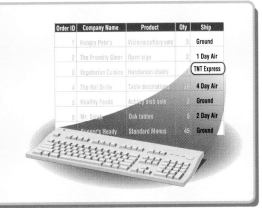

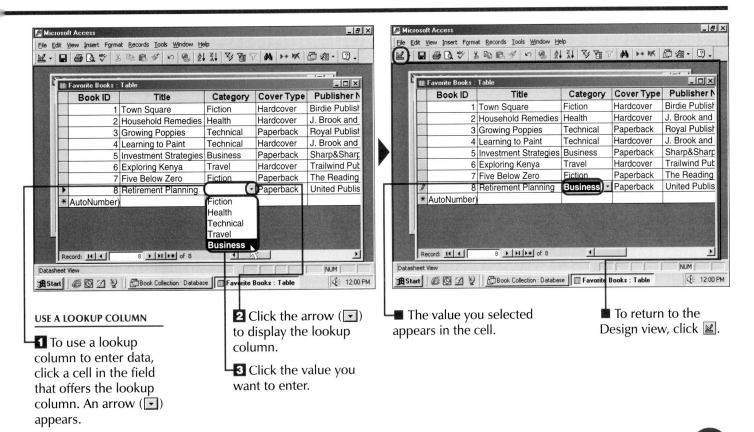

USE A LOOKUP COLUMN

1 To use a lookup column to enter data, click a cell in the field that offers the lookup column. An arrow (▼) appears.

2 Click the arrow (▼) to display the lookup column.

3 Click the value you want to enter.

■ The value you selected appears in the cell.

■ To return to the Design view, click ⊠.

CREATE AN INPUT MASK

You can create an input mask to limit the type of information you can enter in a field. Input masks reduce errors and ensure data has a consistent appearance.

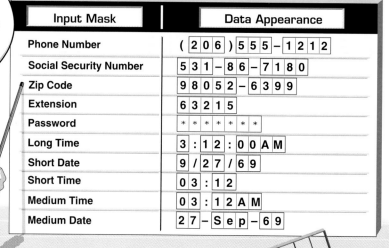

Input Mask	Data Appearance
Phone Number	(2 0 6) 5 5 5 – 1 2 1 2
Social Security Number	5 3 1 – 8 6 – 7 1 8 0
Zip Code	9 8 0 5 2 – 6 3 9 9
Extension	6 3 2 1 5
Password	* * * * * * *
Long Time	3 : 1 2 : 0 0 A M
Short Date	9 / 2 7 / 6 9
Short Time	0 3 : 1 2
Medium Time	0 3 : 1 2 A M
Medium Date	2 7 – S e p – 6 9

The Input Mask Wizard provides common input masks that you can choose from.

CREATE AN INPUT MASK

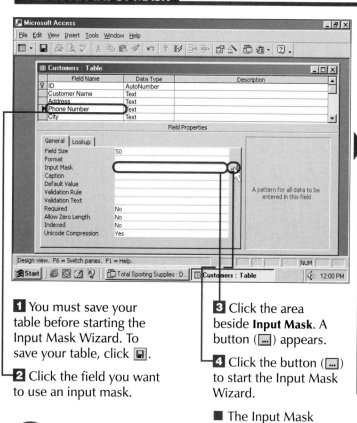

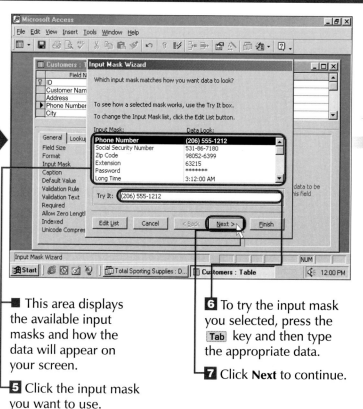

1 You must save your table before starting the Input Mask Wizard. To save your table, click 💾.

2 Click the field you want to use an input mask.

3 Click the area beside **Input Mask**. A button (...) appears.

4 Click the button (...) to start the Input Mask Wizard.

■ The Input Mask Wizard appears.

■ This area displays the available input masks and how the data will appear on your screen.

5 Click the input mask you want to use.

6 To try the input mask you selected, press the Tab key and then type the appropriate data.

7 Click **Next** to continue.

Why does an error message appear when I try to use the Input Mask Wizard?

The Input Mask Wizard is not installed on your computer. Insert the CD-ROM disc you used to install Access into your CD-ROM drive and then click **Yes** to install the wizard.

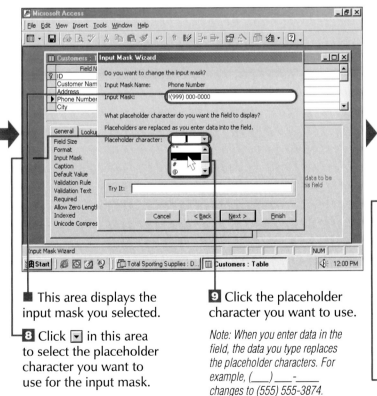

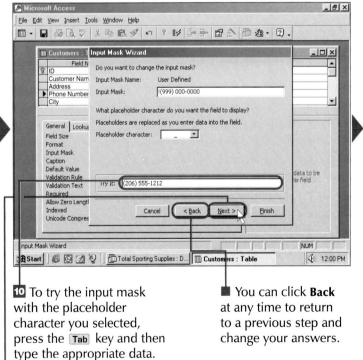

■ This area displays the input mask you selected.

8 Click ▾ in this area to select the placeholder character you want to use for the input mask.

9 Click the placeholder character you want to use.

Note: When you enter data in the field, the data you type replaces the placeholder characters. For example, (___)___-____ changes to (555) 555-3874.

10 To try the input mask with the placeholder character you selected, press the Tab key and then type the appropriate data.

11 Click **Next** to continue.

■ You can click **Back** at any time to return to a previous step and change your answers.

CONTINUED

CREATE AN INPUT MASK

When creating an input mask, the wizard may ask how you want to store the data you enter in the field.

You can store data with or without symbols. Storing data without symbols saves storage space on your computer.

CREATE AN INPUT MASK (CONTINUED)

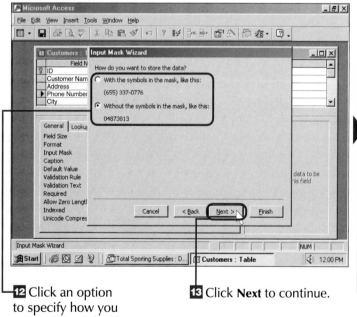

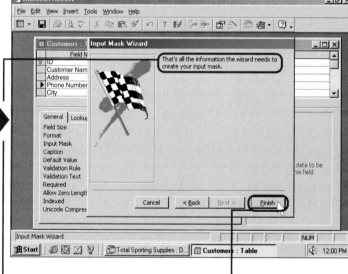

12 Click an option to specify how you want to store the data (○ changes to ⊙).

Note: This screen does not appear for some input masks.

13 Click **Next** to continue.

■ A message appears, indicating that you have finished creating your input mask.

14 Click **Finish**.

TIP

How can an input mask save me time when entering data in a field?

Input masks can save you time by automatically entering characters for you, such as slashes (/) and hyphens (-). For example, when you type 1115551212 in a field that uses the Phone Number input mask, Access will change the data to (111) 555-1212.

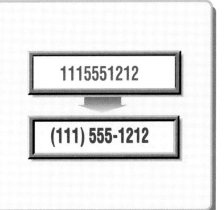

1115551212

(111) 555-1212

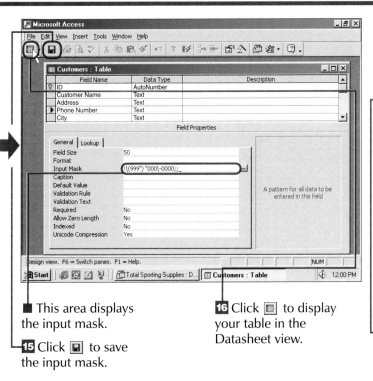

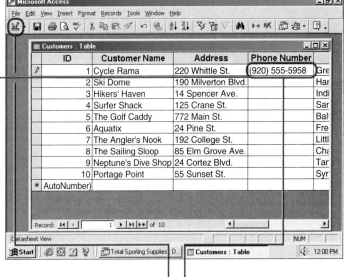

■ This area displays the input mask.

15 Click 🖫 to save the input mask.

16 Click 🖩 to display your table in the Datasheet view.

USE AN INPUT MASK

1 Click an empty cell in the field that uses the input mask. Then press the Home key to move to the beginning of the cell.

2 Type the appropriate data. Access will only accept characters specified by the input mask. For example, you can only enter numbers in a field that uses the Phone Number input mask.

■ To return to the Design view, click 🖾.

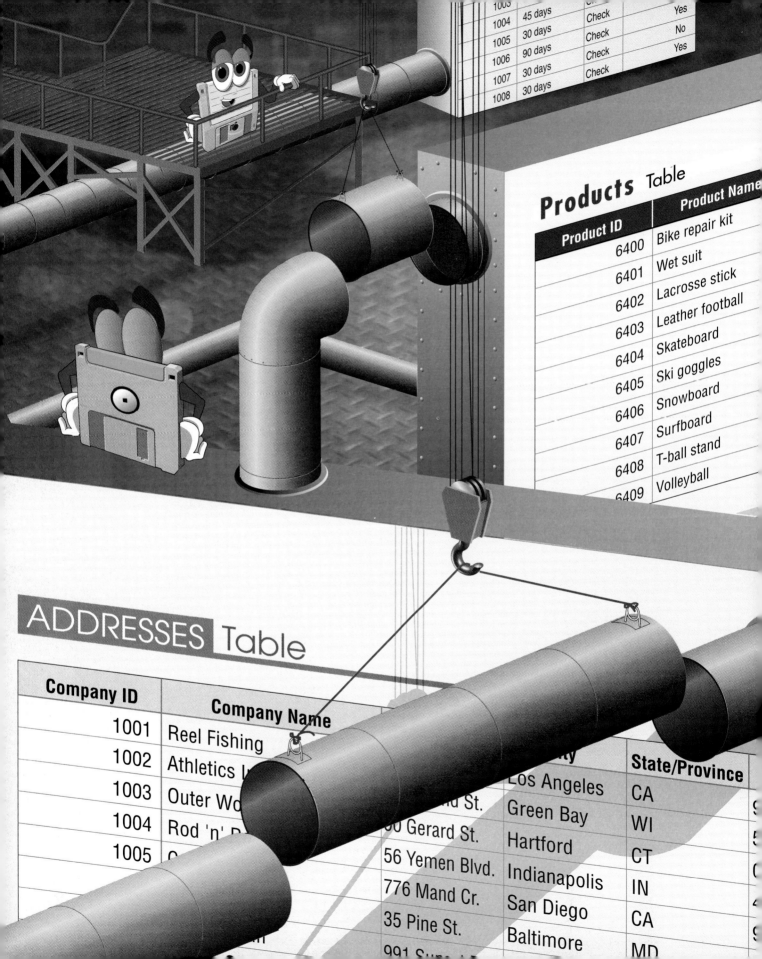

	45 days	Check	Yes
1003			
1004	45 days	Check	No
1005	30 days	Check	Yes
1006	90 days	Check	
1007	30 days	Check	
1008	30 days	Check	

Products Table

Product ID	Product Name
6400	Bike repair kit
6401	Wet suit
6402	Lacrosse stick
6403	Leather football
6404	Skateboard
6405	Ski goggles
6406	Snowboard
6407	Surfboard
6408	T-ball stand
6409	Volleyball

ADDRESSES Table

Company ID	Company Name		City	State/Province	
1001	Reel Fishing		Los Angeles	CA	9
1002	Athletics L	nd St.	Green Bay	WI	5
1003	Outer Wo	0 Gerard St.	Hartford	CT	0
1004	Rod 'n' R	56 Yemen Blvd.	Indianapolis	IN	
1005	C	776 Mand Cr.	San Diego	CA	4
		35 Pine St.	Baltimore	MD	

Price	Units in Stock	Discontinued
		No
	550	No
$34.95	100	No
$389.95	1000	No
$39.95	1500	No
$29.50	500	No
$54.95	700	No
$29.99	150	No
$10.50	100	No
$99.99	100	No
$19.95	750	No
$29.95		

ode

ESTABLISH RELATIONSHIPS

**Are you ready to establish relationships
between the tables in your database?
This chapter teaches you how.**

SET THE PRIMARY KEY

A primary key is one or more fields that uniquely identifies each record in a table. Each table in your database should have a primary key.

You should not change the primary key in a table that has a relationship with another table in your database. For information on relationships, see page 104.

SET THE PRIMARY KEY

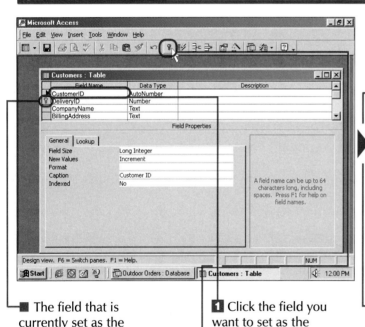

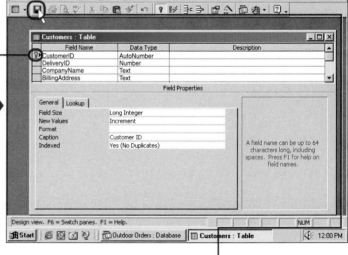

■ The field that is currently set as the primary key displays a key symbol (🔑).

Note: You may have had Access set a primary key for you when you created the table.

1 Click the field you want to set as the primary key.

2 Click 🔑 to set the field as the primary key.

■ A key symbol (🔑) appears beside the field.

3 Click 🖫 to save your change.

102

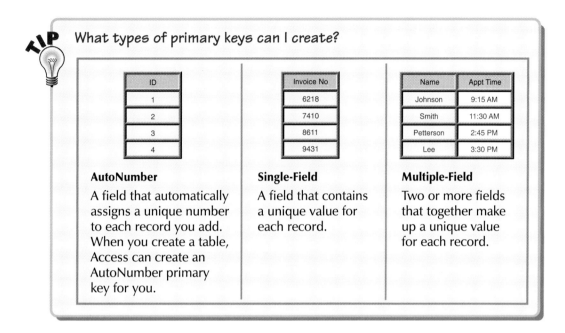

What types of primary keys can I create?

ID
1
2
3
4

Invoice No
6218
7410
8611
9431

Name	Appt Time
Johnson	9:15 AM
Smith	11:30 AM
Petterson	2:45 PM
Lee	3:30 PM

AutoNumber

A field that automatically assigns a unique number to each record you add. When you create a table, Access can create an AutoNumber primary key for you.

Single-Field

A field that contains a unique value for each record.

Multiple-Field

Two or more fields that together make up a unique value for each record.

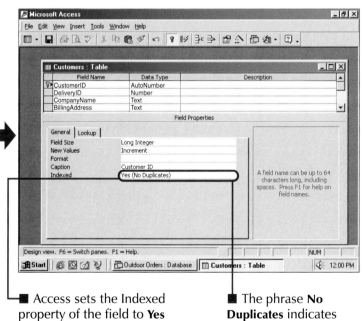

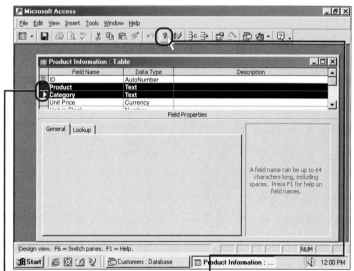

■ Access sets the Indexed property of the field to **Yes (No Duplicates)**. Access will index the data in the field so you can quickly sort and search for data in the field.

■ The phrase **No Duplicates** indicates that Access will not allow you to enter the same value in the field more than once.

You can set more than one field as the primary key.

1 Press and hold down the **Ctrl** key.

2 Still holding down the **Ctrl** key, click the area to the left of each field you want to set as the primary key.

3 Click 🔑 to set the fields as the primary key.

■ A key symbol (🔑) appears beside each field.

CREATE RELATIONSHIPS BETWEEN TABLES

You can create relationships between tables. Relationships allow you to bring together related information in your database.

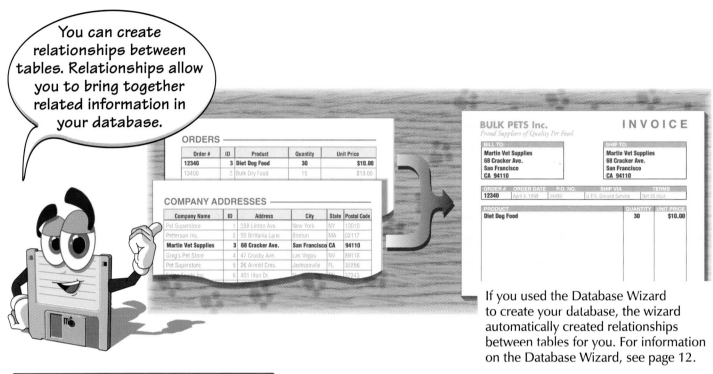

If you used the Database Wizard to create your database, the wizard automatically created relationships between tables for you. For information on the Database Wizard, see page 12.

CREATE RELATIONSHIPS BETWEEN TABLES

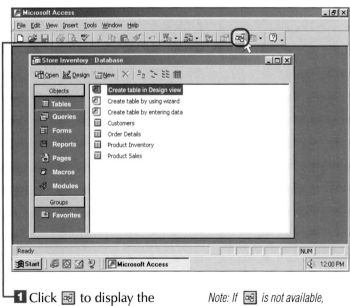

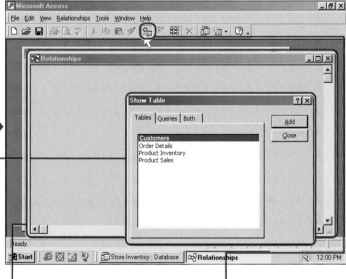

■1 Click 🔲 to display the Relationships window.

Note: If 🔲 is not available, display the Database window. To display the Database window, press the **F11** *key.*

■ The Relationships window appears. If any relationships exist between the tables in your database, a box for each table appears in the window.

■ The Show Table dialog box may also appear, listing all the tables in your database.

■2 If the Show Table dialog box does not appear, click 🔲 to display the dialog box.

Why do I need to create relationships between the tables in my database?

Relationships between tables are essential for creating a form, report or query that uses information from more than one table in your database.

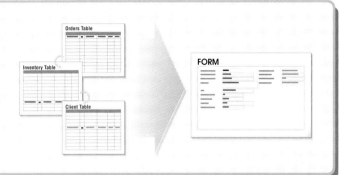

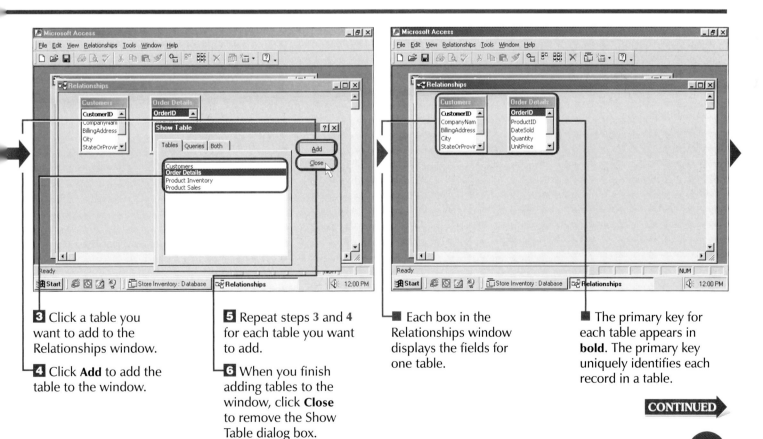

3 Click a table you want to add to the Relationships window.

4 Click **Add** to add the table to the window.

5 Repeat steps 3 and 4 for each table you want to add.

6 When you finish adding tables to the window, click **Close** to remove the Show Table dialog box.

■ Each box in the Relationships window displays the fields for one table.

■ The primary key for each table appears in **bold**. The primary key uniquely identifies each record in a table.

CONTINUED

You create a relationship between tables by identifying the matching fields in the tables.

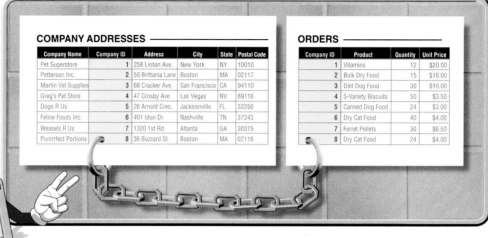

You will usually relate the primary key in one table to a matching field in the other table. In most cases, the fields will have the same name.

CREATE RELATIONSHIPS BETWEEN TABLES (CONTINUED)

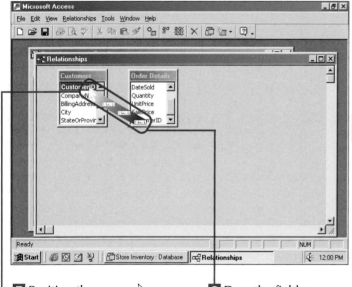

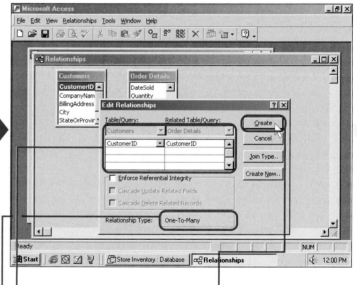

7 Position the mouse ⌖ over the field you want to use to create a relationship with another table.

8 Drag the field over the other table until a small box appears over the matching field.

■ The Edit Relationships dialog box appears.

■ This area displays the names of the tables you are creating a relationship between and the names of the matching fields.

■ This area displays the type of relationship. For more information, see the top of page 107.

9 Click **Create** to create the relationship.

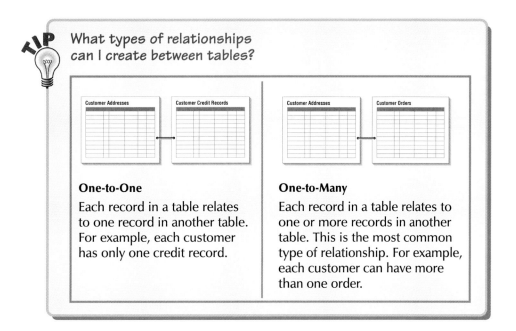

TIP

What types of relationships can I create between tables?

One-to-One

Each record in a table relates to one record in another table. For example, each customer has only one credit record.

One-to-Many

Each record in a table relates to one or more records in another table. This is the most common type of relationship. For example, each customer can have more than one order.

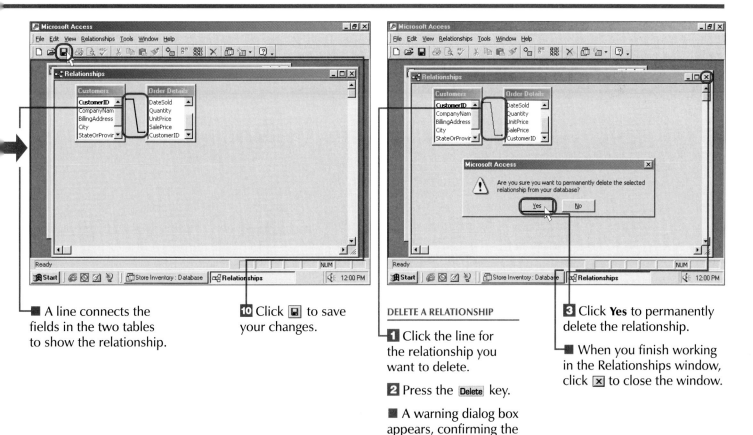

■ A line connects the fields in the two tables to show the relationship.

10 Click 🖫 to save your changes.

DELETE A RELATIONSHIP

1 Click the line for the relationship you want to delete.

2 Press the Delete key.

■ A warning dialog box appears, confirming the deletion.

3 Click **Yes** to permanently delete the relationship.

■ When you finish working in the Relationships window, click ✕ to close the window.

CHAPTER 7

CREATE FORMS

Would you like to use forms to work with data in your database? This chapter teaches you how to present information in an easy-to-use format so you can quickly view, enter and change data.

Justified

CustomerID	Company Name	
2	Big League Inc.	
Billing Address		
423 Idon Dr.		
City	State/Province	Postal Code
Nashville	TN	37243

You can use the AutoForm Wizard to quickly create a form that displays the information from a table in your database.

A form presents data from a table in an attractive, easy-to-use format.

CREATE A FORM USING AN AUTOFORM

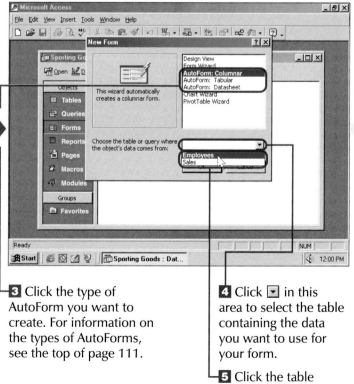

1 Click **Forms** in the Database window.

2 Click **New**.

■ The New Form dialog box appears.

3 Click the type of AutoForm you want to create. For information on the types of AutoForms, see the top of page 111.

4 Click ▼ in this area to select the table containing the data you want to use for your form.

5 Click the table containing the data.

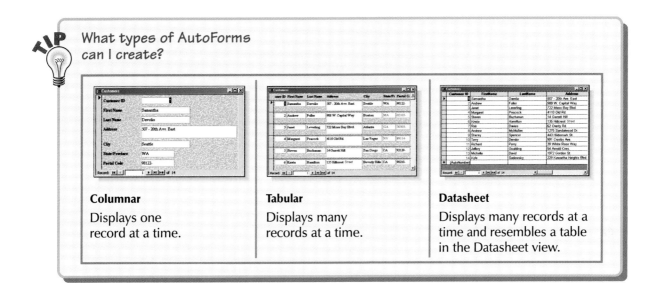

What types of AutoForms can I create?

Columnar

Displays one record at a time.

Tabular

Displays many records at a time.

Datasheet

Displays many records at a time and resembles a table in the Datasheet view.

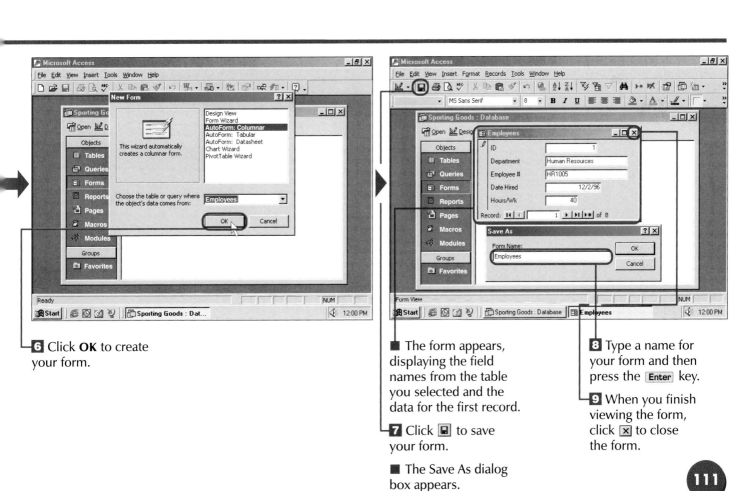

-6 Click **OK** to create your form.

■ The form appears, displaying the field names from the table you selected and the data for the first record.

-7 Click 🖫 to save your form.

■ The Save As dialog box appears.

-8 Type a name for your form and then press the `Enter` key.

-9 When you finish viewing the form, click 🗙 to close the form.

CREATE A FORM USING THE FORM WIZARD

You can use the Form Wizard to help you create a form. The wizard asks you a series of questions and then sets up a form based on your answers.

CREATE A FORM FROM ONE TABLE

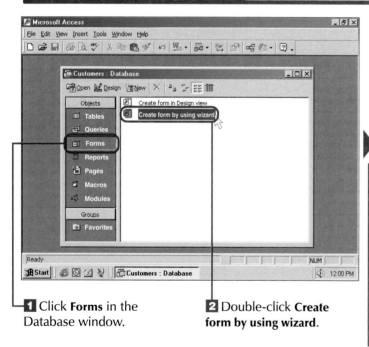

1 Click **Forms** in the Database window.

2 Double-click **Create form by using wizard**.

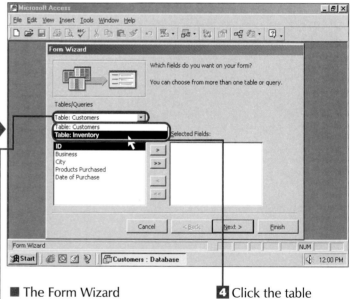

■ The Form Wizard appears.

3 Click ▼ in this area to select the table containing the fields you want to include in your form.

4 Click the table containing the fields.

How can a form help me work with the data in my database?

A form presents data from a table in an attractive, easy-to-use format. You can use a form to view, enter and change data in a table. Many people find forms easier to work with than tables.

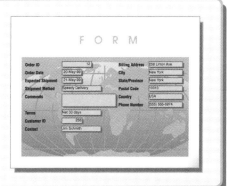

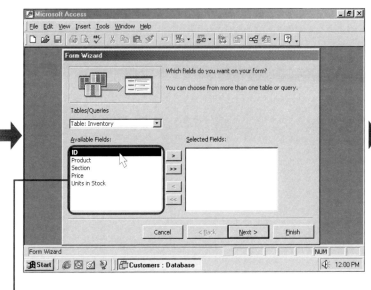

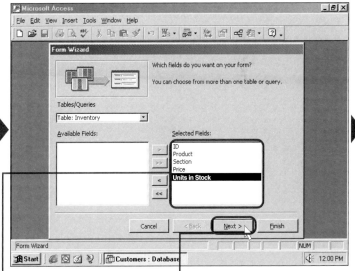

- This area displays the fields from the table you selected.

5 Double-click each field you want to include in your form.

Note: To add all the fields at once, click [≫].

- Each field you select appears in this area.

6 To remove a field you accidentally selected, double-click the field in this area.

Note: To remove all the fields at once, click [≪].

7 When you finish selecting all the fields you want to include in your form, click **Next** to continue.

CONTINUED

113

When creating a form, you can choose between several layouts for your form. The layout of a form determines the arrangement of information on the form.

CREATE A FORM FROM ONE TABLE (CONTINUED)

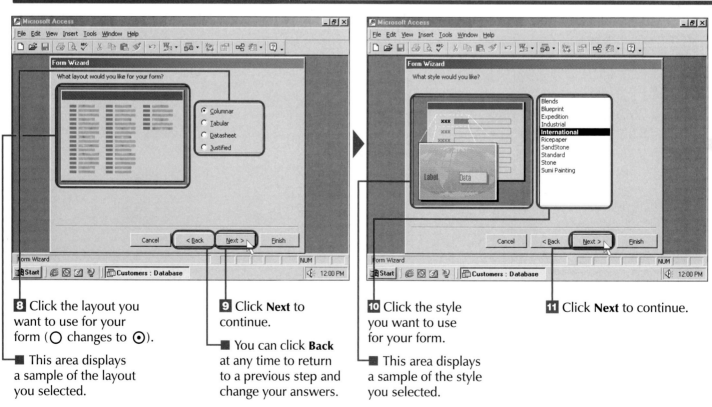

8 Click the layout you want to use for your form (○ changes to ⊙).

■ This area displays a sample of the layout you selected.

9 Click **Next** to continue.

■ You can click **Back** at any time to return to a previous step and change your answers.

10 Click the style you want to use for your form.

■ This area displays a sample of the style you selected.

11 Click **Next** to continue.

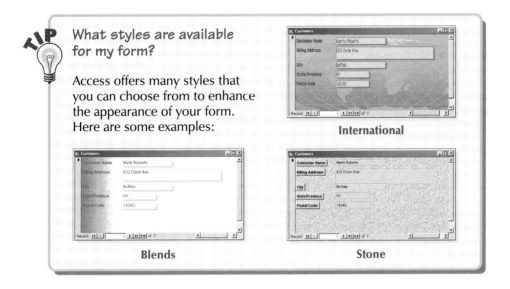

TIP

What styles are available for my form?

Access offers many styles that you can choose from to enhance the appearance of your form. Here are some examples:

International

Blends

Stone

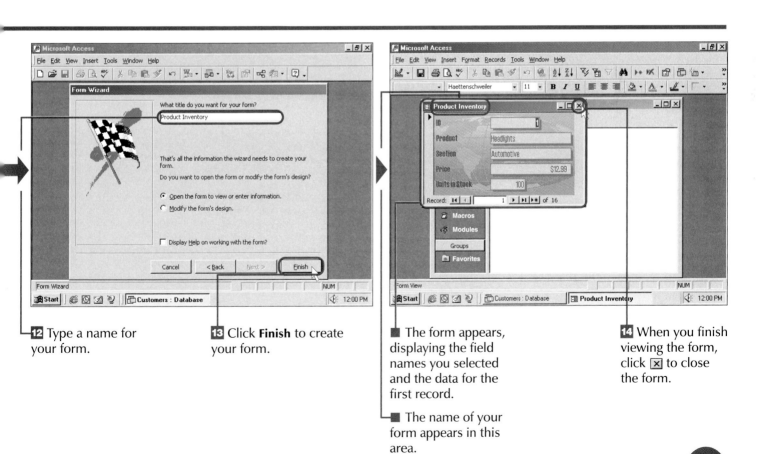

■12 Type a name for your form.

■13 Click **Finish** to create your form.

■ The form appears, displaying the field names you selected and the data for the first record.

■ The name of your form appears in this area.

■14 When you finish viewing the form, click ☒ to close the form.

115

You can use the Form Wizard to create a form that displays information from more than one table in your database.

CREATE A FORM FROM MULTIPLE TABLES

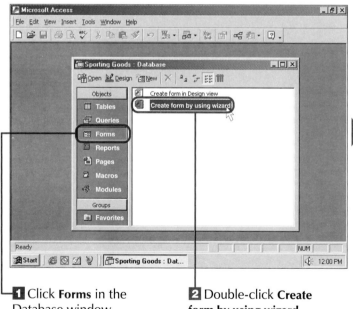

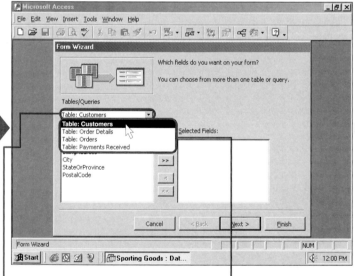

1 Click **Forms** in the Database window.

2 Double-click **Create form by using wizard**.

■ The Form Wizard appears.

3 Click ⏷ in this area to select a table containing fields you want to include in your form.

4 Click the table containing the fields.

Which tables in my database can I use to create a form?

You can use any table in your database to create a form. To create a form using data from more than one table, relationships must exist between the tables. For information on relationships, see page 104.

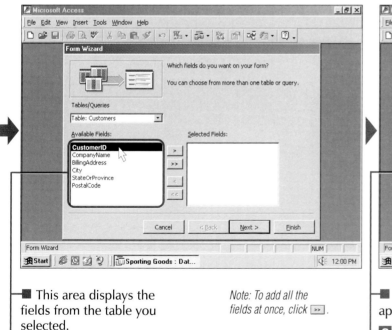

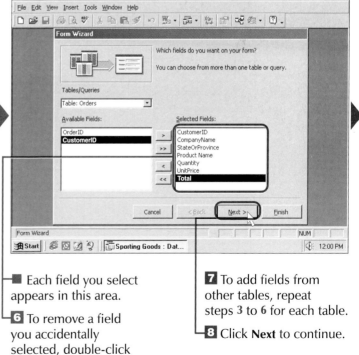

■ This area displays the fields from the table you selected.

5 Double-click each field you want to include in your form.

Note: To add all the fields at once, click ▦.

■ Each field you select appears in this area.

6 To remove a field you accidentally selected, double-click the field in this area.

Note: To remove all the fields at once, click ◄◄.

7 To add fields from other tables, repeat steps **3** to **6** for each table.

8 Click **Next** to continue.

CONTINUED

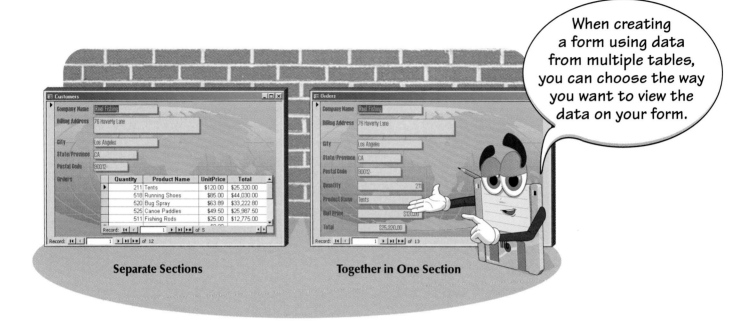

When creating a form using data from multiple tables, you can choose the way you want to view the data on your form.

Separate Sections

Together in One Section

CREATE A FORM FROM MULTIPLE TABLES (CONTINUED)

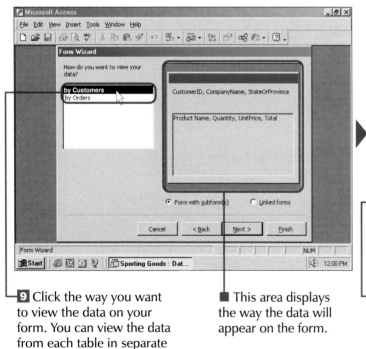

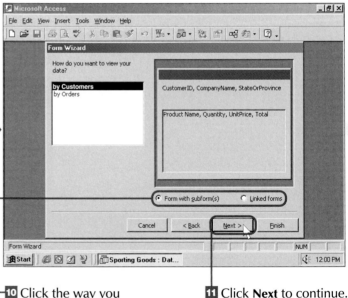

9 Click the way you want to view the data on your form. You can view the data from each table in separate sections or together in one section.

■ This area displays the way the data will appear on the form.

10 Click the way you want to organize the data (○ changes to ⊙). For more information, see the top of page 119.

Note: These options are not available if you chose to view the data from each table in one section in step 9.

11 Click **Next** to continue.

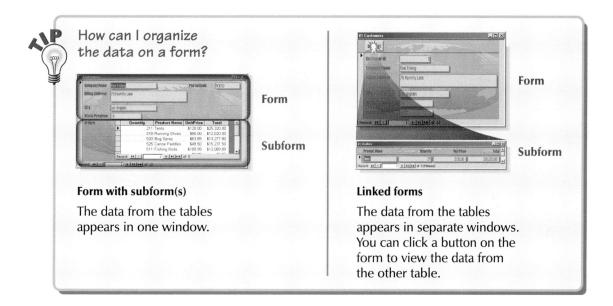

TIP

How can I organize the data on a form?

Form with subform(s)

The data from the tables appears in one window.

Linked forms

The data from the tables appears in separate windows. You can click a button on the form to view the data from the other table.

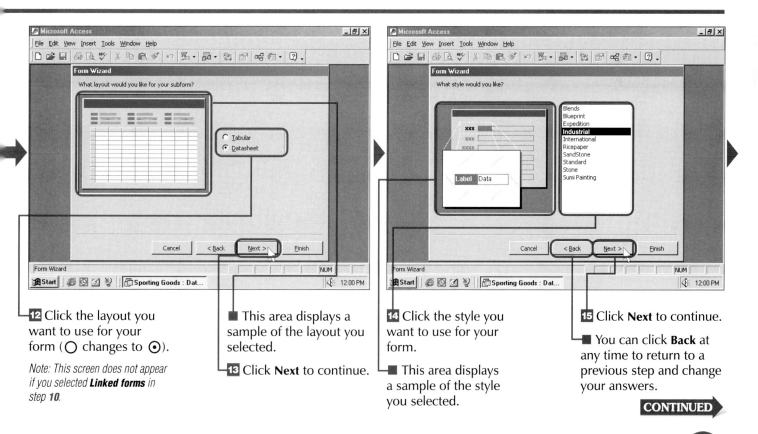

12 Click the layout you want to use for your form (○ changes to ◉).

*Note: This screen does not appear if you selected **Linked forms** in step **10**.*

■ This area displays a sample of the layout you selected.

13 Click **Next** to continue.

14 Click the style you want to use for your form.

■ This area displays a sample of the style you selected.

15 Click **Next** to continue.

■ You can click **Back** at any time to return to a previous step and change your answers.

CONTINUED ▶

CREATE A FORM USING THE FORM WIZARD

You can give your form a descriptive name. If your form contains a subform, you can also name the subform.

Main Form

Subform

CREATE A FORM FROM MULTIPLE TABLES (CONTINUED)

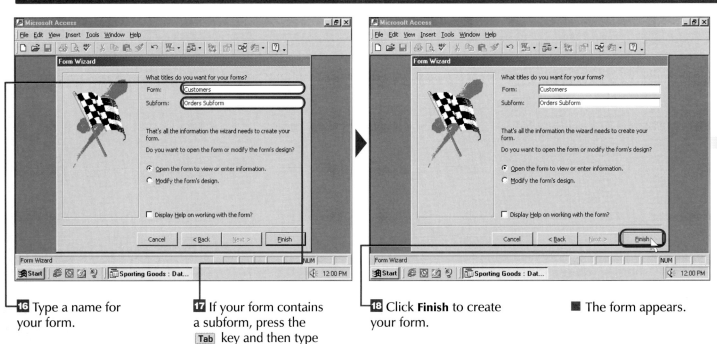

16 Type a name for your form.

17 If your form contains a subform, press the `Tab` key and then type a name for the subform.

18 Click **Finish** to create your form.

■ The form appears.

120

How will my new form appear in the Database window?

If you created a form that contains a subform, both the main form and subform will be listed in the Database window. You must open the main form to work with the contents of both the main form and the subform.

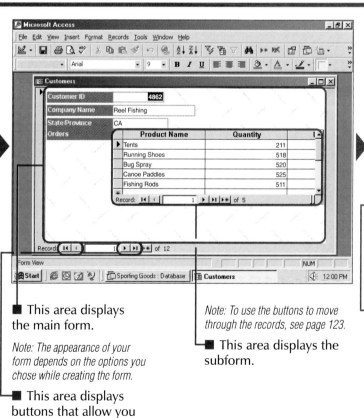

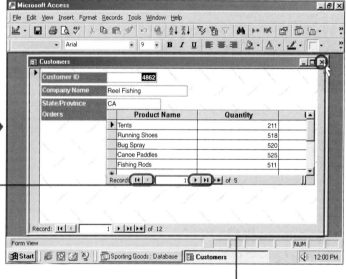

■ This area displays the main form.

Note: The appearance of your form depends on the options you chose while creating the form.

■ This area displays buttons that allow you to move through the records in the main form.

Note: To use the buttons to move through the records, see page 123.

■ This area displays the subform.

■ This area displays buttons that allow you to move through the records in the subform.

■ As you move through the records in the main form, the information in the subform changes. For example, when you display the name and address of a customer, the orders for the customer appear in the subform.

19 When you finish viewing the form, click ☒ to close the form.

OPEN A FORM

You can open a form to display its contents on your screen. This lets you review and make changes to the form.

OPEN A FORM

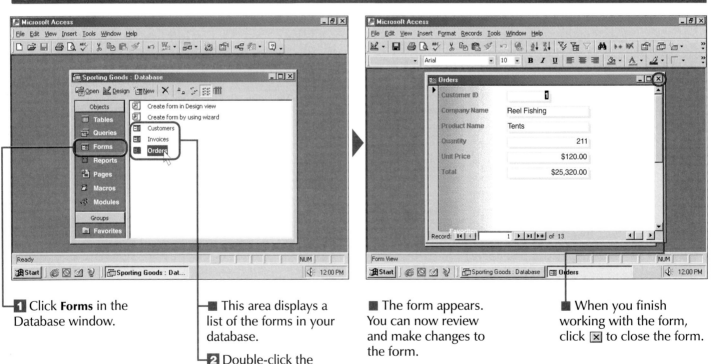

1 Click **Forms** in the Database window.

■ This area displays a list of the forms in your database.

2 Double-click the form you want to open.

■ The form appears. You can now review and make changes to the form.

■ When you finish working with the form, click ☒ to close the form.

122

MOVE THROUGH RECORDS

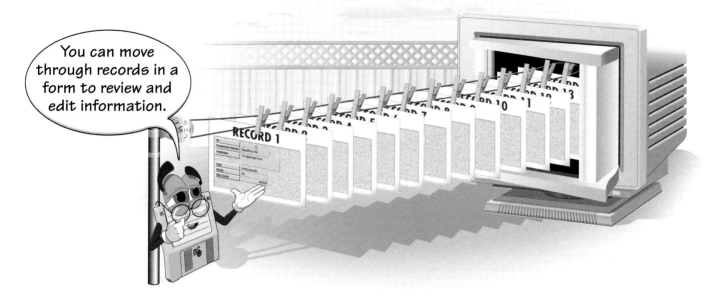

You can move through records in a form to review and edit information.

MOVE THROUGH RECORDS

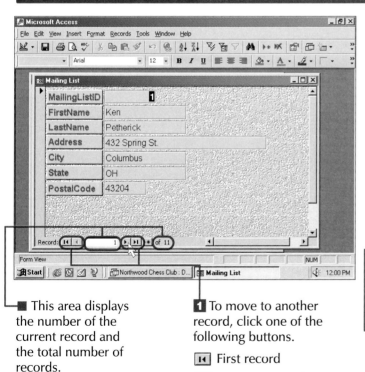

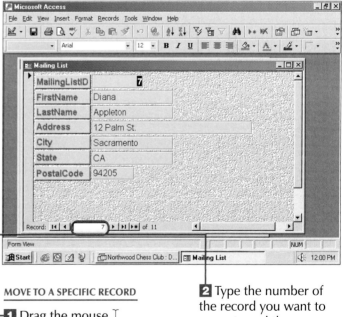

■ This area displays the number of the current record and the total number of records.

1 To move to another record, click one of the following buttons.

⏮ First record

◀ Previous record

▶ Next record

⏭ Last record

MOVE TO A SPECIFIC RECORD

1 Drag the mouse I over the number of the current record. The number is highlighted.

2 Type the number of the record you want to move to and then press the **Enter** key.

123

You can edit the data in a form to correct a mistake or update the data.

Access automatically saves the changes you make to the data in a form.

When you change data in a form, Access will also change the data in the table you used to create the form.

EDIT DATA

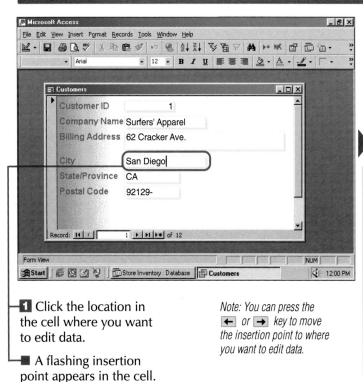

1 Click the location in the cell where you want to edit data.

■ A flashing insertion point appears in the cell.

Note: You can press the ← or → key to move the insertion point to where you want to edit data.

2 To remove the character to the left of the insertion point, press the +Backspace key.

3 To insert data where the insertion point flashes on your screen, type the data.

4 When you finish making changes to the data, press the Enter key.

TIP

Why *does* the existing data disappear when I type new data?

When **OVR** appears in **bold** at the bottom of your screen, the Overtype feature is on. When this feature is on, the data you type will replace the existing data. To turn off the Overtype feature, press the `Insert` key.

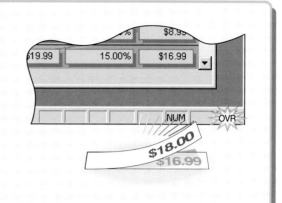

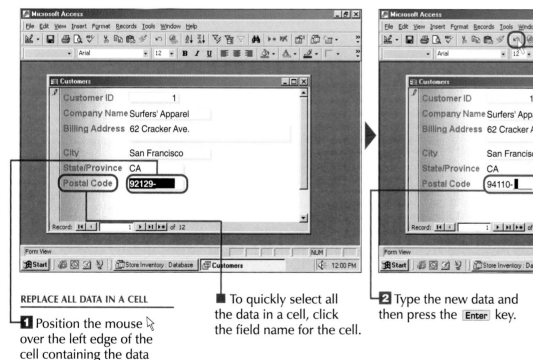

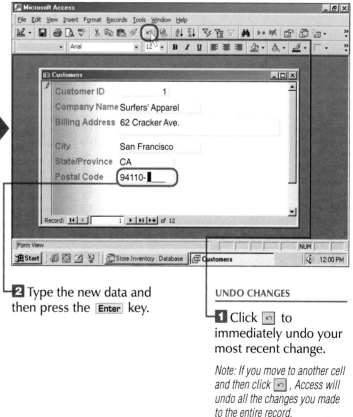

REPLACE ALL DATA IN A CELL

1 Position the mouse � over the left edge of the cell containing the data you want to replace with new data (� changes to I). Then drag the mouse I until you highlight all the data in the cell.

■ To quickly select all the data in a cell, click the field name for the cell.

2 Type the new data and then press the `Enter` key.

UNDO CHANGES

1 Click � to immediately undo your most recent change.

Note: If you move to another cell and then click � , Access will undo all the changes you made to the entire record.

You can add a record to a form to insert new information into your database. For example, you may want to add information about a new customer.

Access automatically saves each new record you add to a form.

When you add a record to a form, Access also adds the record to the table you used to create the form.

ADD A RECORD

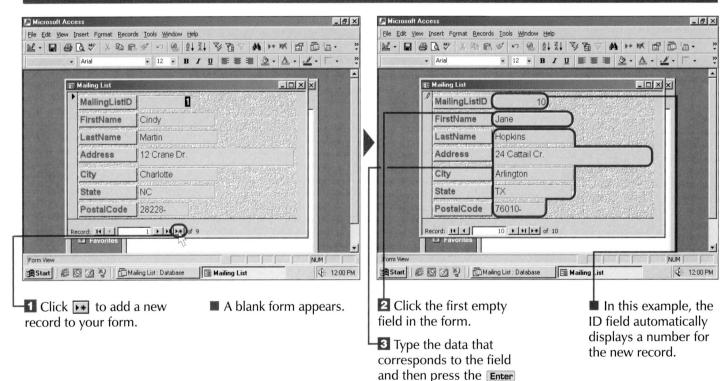

1 Click ►✱ to add a new record to your form.

■ A blank form appears.

2 Click the first empty field in the form.

3 Type the data that corresponds to the field and then press the `Enter` key to move to the next field. Repeat this step until you finish entering all the data for the record.

■ In this example, the ID field automatically displays a number for the new record.

DELETE A RECORD

DELETE A RECORD

You can delete a record to permanently remove information you no longer need. For example, you may want to remove information about a customer who no longer orders your products.

When you delete a record from a form, Access also removes the record from the table you used to create the form.

Deleting records saves storage space on your computer and reduces clutter in your database.

DELETE A RECORD

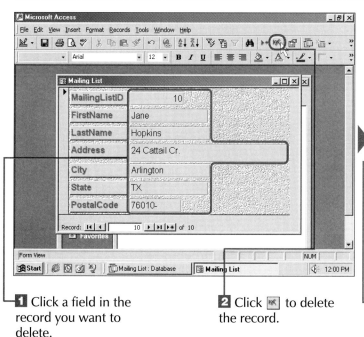

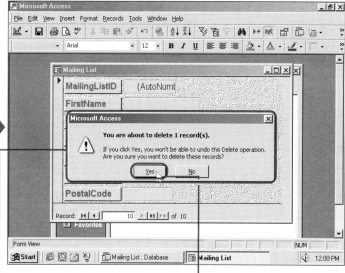

1 Click a field in the record you want to delete.

2 Click ▨ to delete the record.

■ A warning dialog box appears, confirming the deletion.

3 Click **Yes** to permanently delete the record.

■ The record disappears.

There are three ways you can view a form. Each view allows you to perform different tasks.

VIEWS

☐ Design View
☑ Form View
☐ Datasheet View

CHANGE VIEW OF FORM

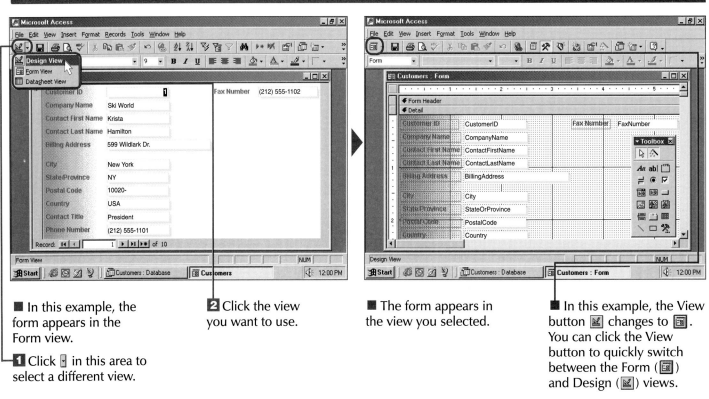

■ In this example, the form appears in the Form view.

1 Click 🔽 in this area to select a different view.

2 Click the view you want to use.

■ The form appears in the view you selected.

■ In this example, the View button 🔲 changes to 🔲. You can click the View button to quickly switch between the Form (🔲) and Design (🔲) views.

THE FORM VIEWS

Design View

The Design view allows you to change the layout and design of a form.

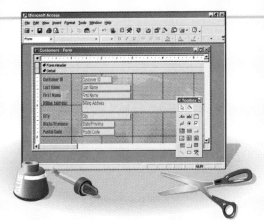

You can customize the form to make it easier to use or to enhance the appearance of the form.

Form View

The Form view usually displays one record at a time in an organized and attractive format.

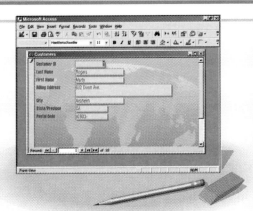

You can use this view to enter, edit and review information.

Datasheet View

The Datasheet view displays all the records in rows and columns.

The field names appear across the top of the window. Each row displays the information for one record. You can enter, edit and review information in this view.

APPLY AN AUTOFORMAT

You can apply an autoformat to quickly change the overall appearance of a form.

APPLY AN AUTOFORMAT

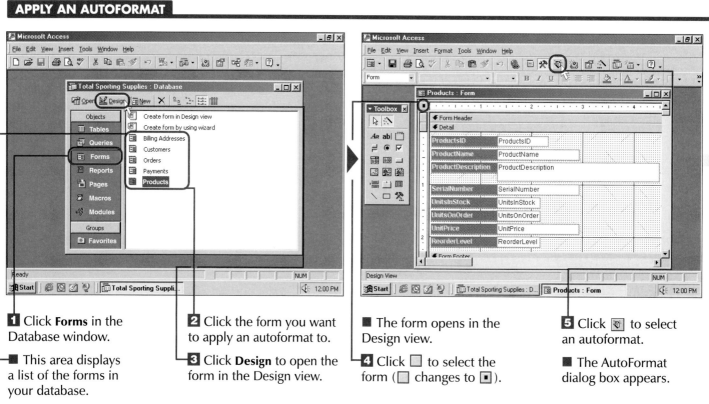

1 Click **Forms** in the Database window.

■ This area displays a list of the forms in your database.

2 Click the form you want to apply an autoformat to.

3 Click **Design** to open the form in the Design view.

■ The form opens in the Design view.

4 Click ☐ to select the form (☐ changes to ▣).

5 Click 🔁 to select an autoformat.

■ The AutoFormat dialog box appears.

Why didn't my entire form change to the new autoformat?

If your form contains a subform, the appearance of the subform will not change when you apply an autoformat to the form. To change the appearance of the subform, perform steps **1** to **8** below, selecting the subform in step **2**.

Note: If your subform appears in the Datasheet layout, you cannot change the appearance of the subform. A subform in the Datasheet layout looks like a table.

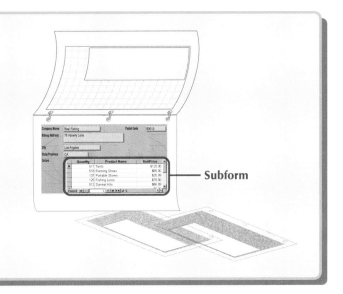

Subform

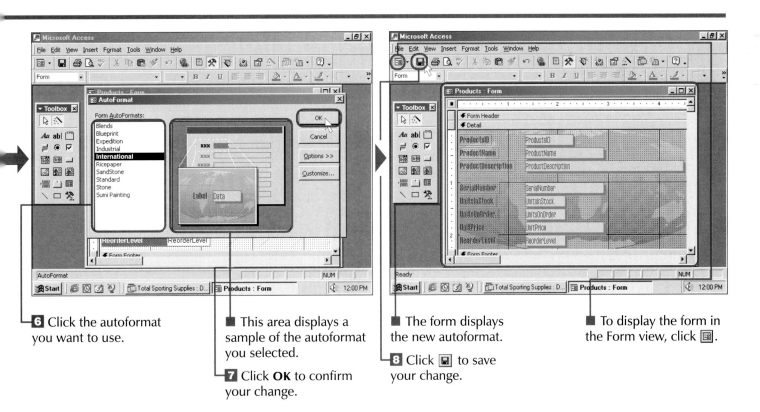

■6 Click the autoformat you want to use.

■ This area displays a sample of the autoformat you selected.

■7 Click **OK** to confirm your change.

■ The form displays the new autoformat.

■8 Click 🖫 to save your change.

■ To display the form in the Form view, click 🗊.

CHAPTER 8

FIND DATA

Would you like to learn how to find specific data in your database? This chapter teaches you how to find, sort and filter the data in your tables, forms and queries.

SORT RECORDS

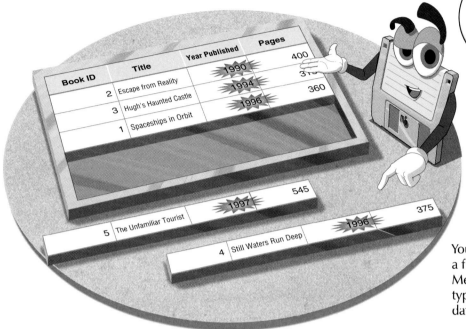

You can change the order of records in a table, query or form. This can help you find, organize and analyze data.

You cannot sort data in a field with the Hyperlink, Memo or OLE Object data type. For information on data types, see page 75.

SORT RECORDS

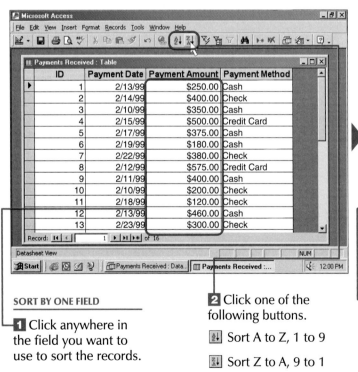

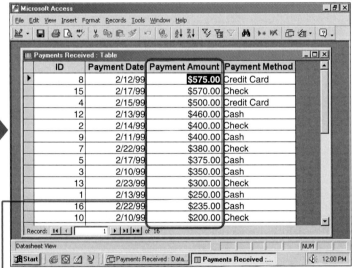

SORT BY ONE FIELD

1 Click anywhere in the field you want to use to sort the records.

2 Click one of the following buttons.

Sort A to Z, 1 to 9

Sort Z to A, 9 to 1

■ The records appear in the new order. In this example, the records are sorted by payment amount.

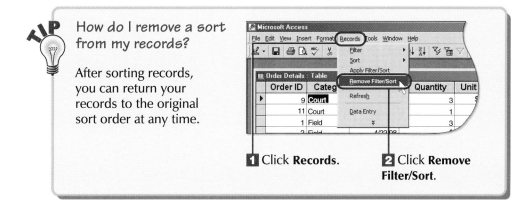

How do I remove a sort from my records?

After sorting records, you can return your records to the original sort order at any time.

1 Click **Records**.

2 Click **Remove Filter/Sort**.

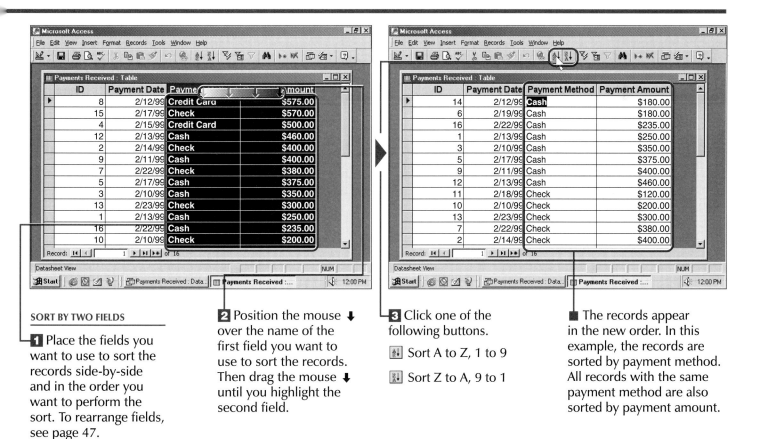

SORT BY TWO FIELDS

1 Place the fields you want to use to sort the records side-by-side and in the order you want to perform the sort. To rearrange fields, see page 47.

2 Position the mouse ↓ over the name of the first field you want to use to sort the records. Then drag the mouse ↓ until you highlight the second field.

3 Click one of the following buttons.

 Sort A to Z, 1 to 9

 Sort Z to A, 9 to 1

■ The records appear in the new order. In this example, the records are sorted by payment method. All records with the same payment method are also sorted by payment amount.

135

FIND DATA

You can search for data of interest in your database.

You can search for data in tables, queries and forms.

FIND DATA

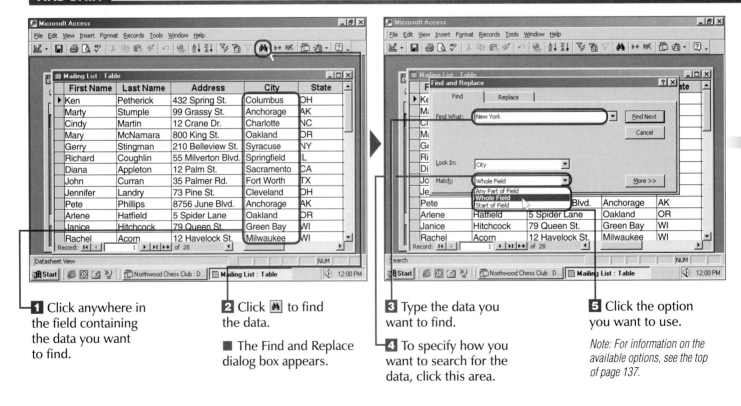

1 Click anywhere in the field containing the data you want to find.

2 Click 🔍 to find the data.

■ The Find and Replace dialog box appears.

3 Type the data you want to find.

4 To specify how you want to search for the data, click this area.

5 Click the option you want to use.

Note: For information on the available options, see the top of page 137.

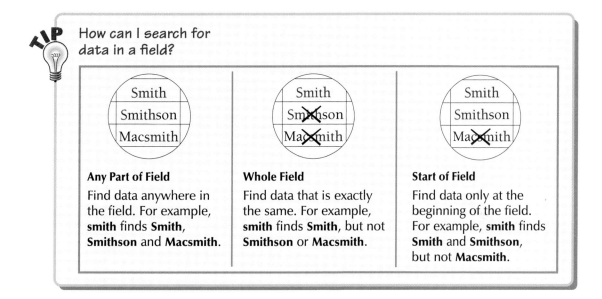

TIP

How can I search for data in a field?

Smith	Smith	Smith
Smithson	~~Smithson~~	Smithson
Macsmith	~~Macsmith~~	~~Macsmith~~

Any Part of Field

Find data anywhere in the field. For example, **smith** finds **Smith**, **Smithson** and **Macsmith**.

Whole Field

Find data that is exactly the same. For example, **smith** finds **Smith**, but not **Smithson** or **Macsmith**.

Start of Field

Find data only at the beginning of the field. For example, **smith** finds **Smith** and **Smithson**, but not **Macsmith**.

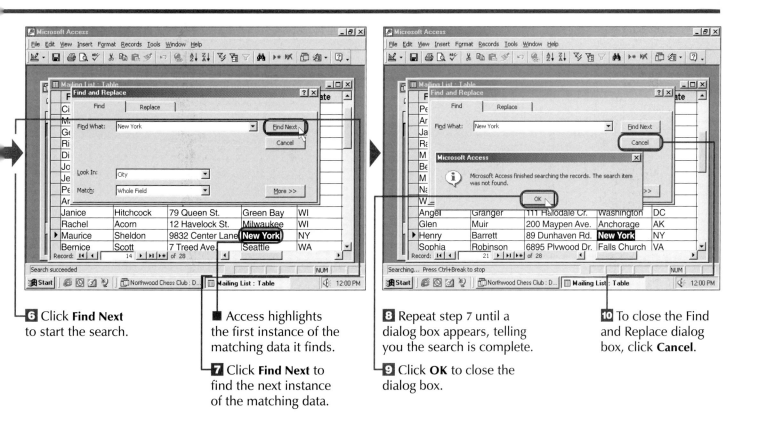

6 Click **Find Next** to start the search.

■ Access highlights the first instance of the matching data it finds.

7 Click **Find Next** to find the next instance of the matching data.

8 Repeat step 7 until a dialog box appears, telling you the search is complete.

9 Click **OK** to close the dialog box.

10 To close the Find and Replace dialog box, click **Cancel**.

You can filter data in a table, form or query to display only records that contain data of interest. This can help you review and analyze information in your database.

For example, you can display only the records for customers living in California.

FILTER BY SELECTION

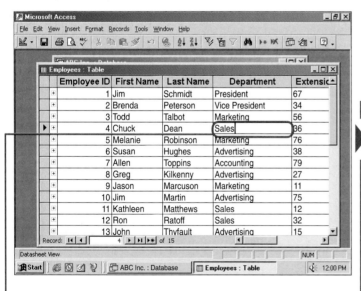

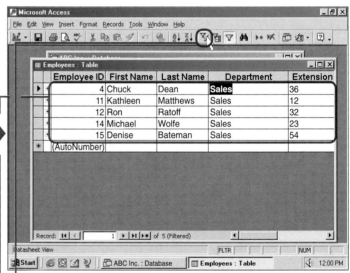

1 Click the data you want to use to filter the records.

Note: You can select data to change the way Access filters the records. For more information, see the top of page 139.

2 Click 📝 to filter the records.

■ Access displays the records containing the data. All other records are hidden.

■ In this example, Access displays employees in the Sales department.

TIP

How can I change the way Access filters records?

You can select data to change the way Access filters records. To select data, see page 55.

Exact Match

If you do not select any data, Access will find data that matches exactly. For example, **Smith** finds only **Smith**.

First Characters

If you select part of the data, starting with the first character, Access will find data that starts with the same characters. For example, **Smi**th finds **Smi**thson and **Smi**ley.

Any Characters

If you select part of the data, starting after the first character, Access will find data containing the selected characters. For example, Ron**son**ville finds **Son**y and Smith**son**.

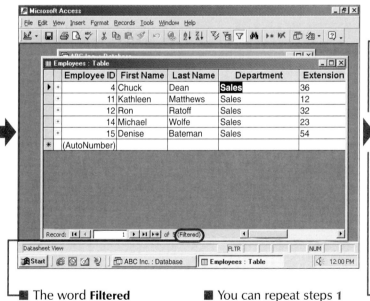

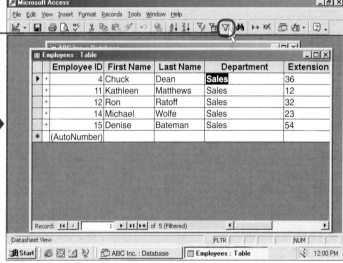

■ The word **Filtered** appears in this area to indicate that you are viewing filtered records.

■ You can repeat steps **1** and **2** to further filter the records.

■3 When you finish reviewing the filtered records, click ⏷ to once again display all the records.

FILTER BY FORM

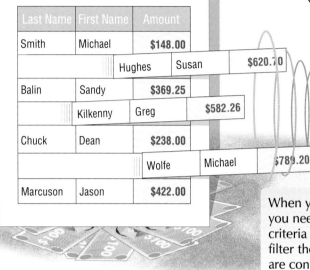

You can use the Filter by Form feature to find and display records of interest in a table, form or query.

When you filter by form, you need to specify the criteria you want to use to filter the records. Criteria are conditions that identify which records you want to display.

For example, you can display customers who purchased more than $500.00 of your product.

FILTER BY FORM USING ONE CRITERIA

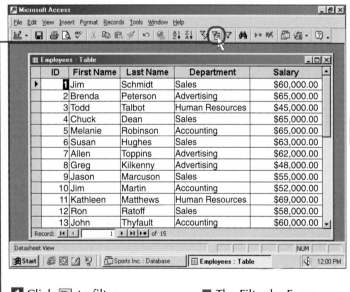

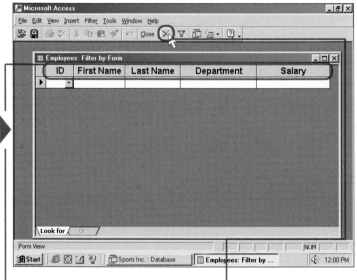

1 Click 🔲 to filter by form.

■ The Filter by Form window appears.

■ This area displays the field names from your table.

2 To clear any criteria used for your last filter, click ☒.

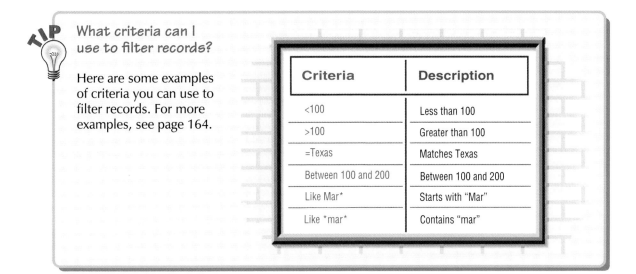

TIP

What criteria can I use to filter records?

Here are some examples of criteria you can use to filter records. For more examples, see page 164.

Criteria	Description
<100	Less than 100
>100	Greater than 100
=Texas	Matches Texas
Between 100 and 200	Between 100 and 200
Like Mar*	Starts with "Mar"
Like *mar*	Contains "mar"

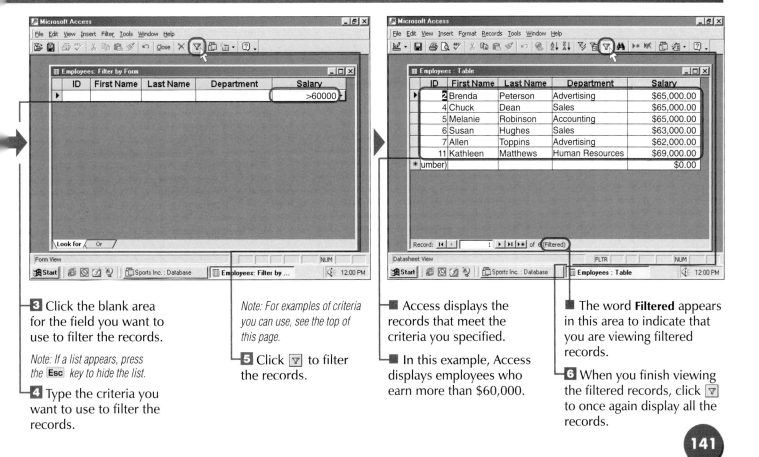

3 Click the blank area for the field you want to use to filter the records.

Note: If a list appears, press the Esc key to hide the list.

4 Type the criteria you want to use to filter the records.

Note: For examples of criteria you can use, see the top of this page.

5 Click 🔽 to filter the records.

■ Access displays the records that meet the criteria you specified.

■ In this example, Access displays employees who earn more than $60,000.

■ The word **Filtered** appears in this area to indicate that you are viewing filtered records.

6 When you finish viewing the filtered records, click 🔽 to once again display all the records.

141

You can use multiple criteria to filter your records. Access will find and display records that meet the criteria you specify.

Criteria are conditions that identify which records you want to display. For examples of criteria, see page 164.

For example, you can display customers living in California who purchased more than $500 of your product.

FILTER BY FORM USING MULTIPLE CRITERIA

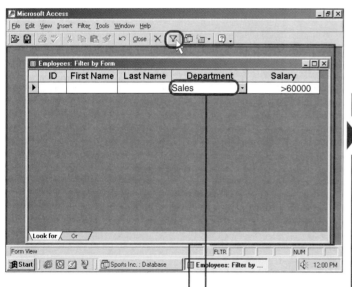

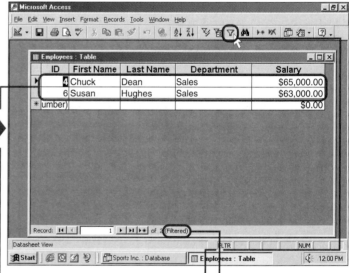

USING "AND"

1 To enter the first criteria you want to use to filter the records, perform steps **1** to **4** starting on page 140.

2 To enter the second criteria, click the blank area for the other field you want to use to filter the records. Then type the second criteria.

3 Click ▽ to filter the records.

■ Access displays the records that meet both of the criteria you specified.

■ In this example, Access displays employees in the Sales department who earn more than $60,000.

■ The word **Filtered** appears in this area to indicate that you are viewing filtered records.

4 When you finish viewing the filtered records, click ▽ to once again display all the records.

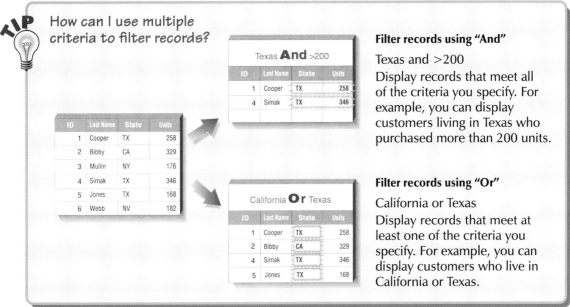

How can I use multiple criteria to filter records?

Filter records using "And"

Texas **And** >200

Texas and >200
Display records that meet all of the criteria you specify. For example, you can display customers living in Texas who purchased more than 200 units.

Filter records using "Or"

California **Or** Texas

California or Texas
Display records that meet at least one of the criteria you specify. For example, you can display customers who live in California or Texas.

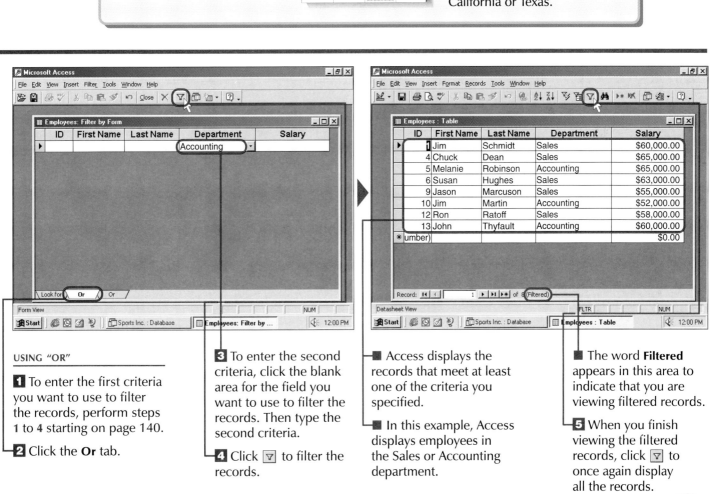

USING "OR"

1 To enter the first criteria you want to use to filter the records, perform steps **1** to **4** starting on page 140.

2 Click the **Or** tab.

3 To enter the second criteria, click the blank area for the field you want to use to filter the records. Then type the second criteria.

4 Click ▼ to filter the records.

■ Access displays the records that meet at least one of the criteria you specified.

■ In this example, Access displays employees in the Sales or Accounting department.

■ The word **Filtered** appears in this area to indicate that you are viewing filtered records.

5 When you finish viewing the filtered records, click ▼ to once again display all the records.

CHAPTER 9

CREATE QUERIES

Are you ready to create queries? This chapter teaches you how to create a query to find information of interest in your database.

What is the lowest

Who is the top

Which product has

Which sales reps sold
the most products
this month?

Queries

You can create a query to find information of interest in your database.

Which wines were made before 1965?

When you create a query, you ask Access to find information that meets certain criteria or conditions.

When creating a query that uses more than one table, the tables should be related. For information on relationships, see page 104.

CREATE A QUERY IN THE DESIGN VIEW

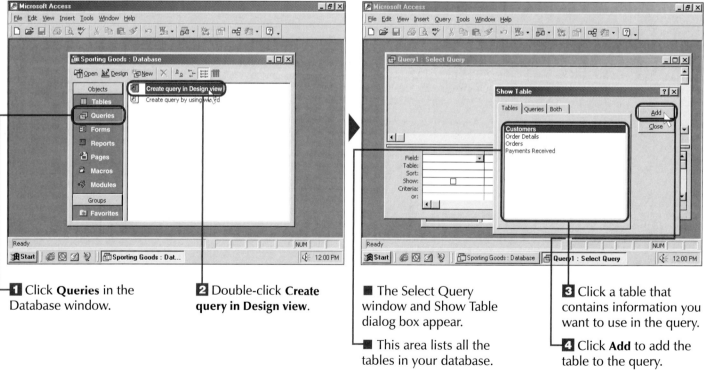

1 Click **Queries** in the Database window.

2 Double-click **Create query in Design view**.

■ The Select Query window and Show Table dialog box appear.

■ This area lists all the tables in your database.

3 Click a table that contains information you want to use in the query.

4 Click **Add** to add the table to the query.

146

How do I add another table to a query?

You can click 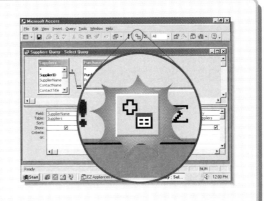 at any time to redisplay the Show Table dialog box and add another table to the query. To add another table to the query, perform steps **3** and **4** on page 146.

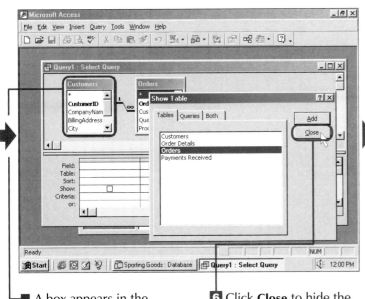

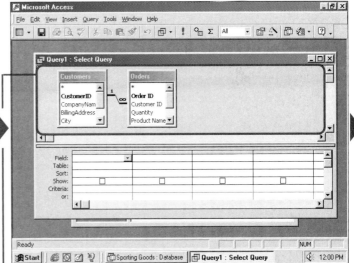

■ A box appears in the Select Query window, displaying the fields for the table you selected.

5 Repeat steps **3** and **4** for each table you want to use in the query.

6 Click **Close** to hide the Show Table dialog box.

■ Each box in this area displays the fields for one table.

Note: If the tables are related, Access displays a line joining the related fields. For information on relationships, see page 104.

■ If you accidentally added a table to the query, click the table and then press the Delete key. This removes the table from the query, but not from the database.

CONTINUED

Query Results

You can select which fields you want to include in your query.

For example, you may want to include only the name and phone number of each customer.

CREATE A QUERY IN THE DESIGN VIEW (CONTINUED)

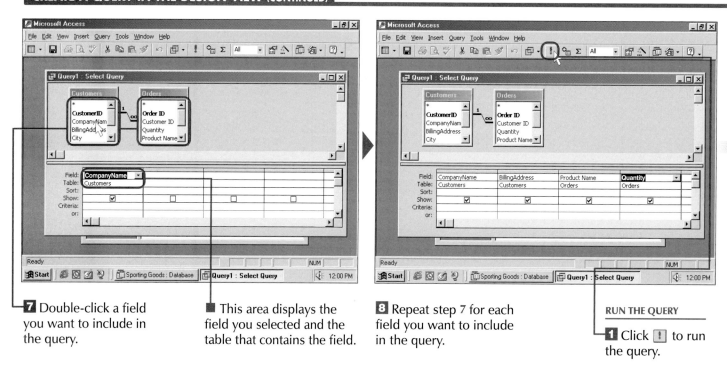

7 Double-click a field you want to include in the query.

■ This area displays the field you selected and the table that contains the field.

8 Repeat step 7 for each field you want to include in the query.

RUN THE QUERY

1 Click 🔲 to run the query.

Does a query store data?

No. When you save a query, Access only saves the design of the query. Each time you run a query, Access gathers the most current data from your database to determine the results of the query. For example, you can run the same query each month to display the top sales representatives for the month.

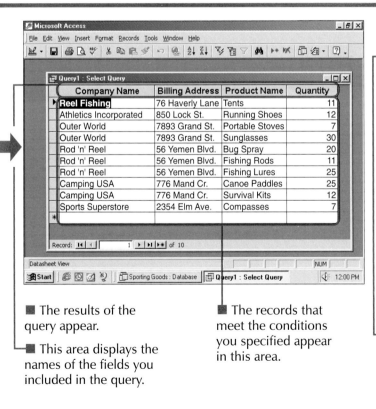

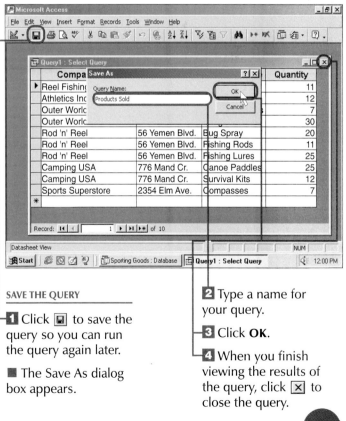

■ The results of the query appear.

■ This area displays the names of the fields you included in the query.

■ The records that meet the conditions you specified appear in this area.

SAVE THE QUERY

1 Click 🔲 to save the query so you can run the query again later.

■ The Save As dialog box appears.

2 Type a name for your query.

3 Click **OK**.

4 When you finish viewing the results of the query, click ✖ to close the query.

You can use the Simple Query Wizard to create a query. A query allows you to find information of interest in your database.

The Simple Query Wizard will ask you a series of questions and then sct up a query based on your answers.

CREATE A QUERY USING THE SIMPLE QUERY WIZARD

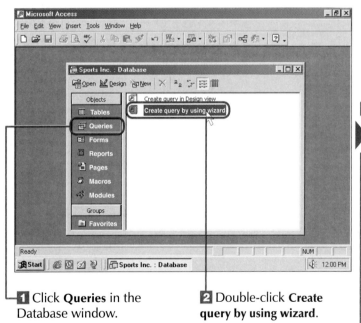

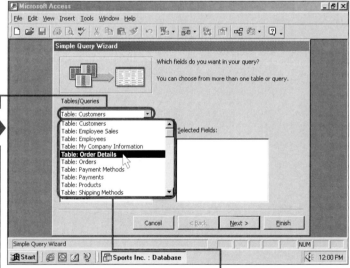

1 Click **Queries** in the Database window.

2 Double-click **Create query by using wizard**.

■ The Simple Query Wizard appears.

3 Click ▾ in this area to select the table containing the fields you want to include in your query.

4 Click the table containing the fields.

Which tables in my database can I use to create a query?

You can use any table in your database to create a query. To create a query using data from more than one table, relationships must exist between the tables. For information on relationships, see page 104.

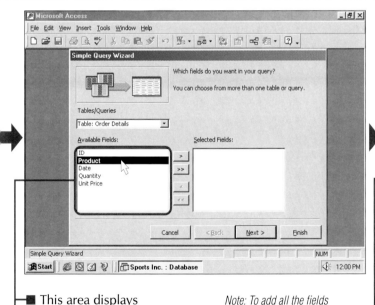

■ This area displays the fields from the table you selected.

Note: To add all the fields at once, click ▶▶ *.*

5 Double-click each field you want to include in your query.

■ Each field you select appears in this area.

■ To remove a field you accidentally selected, double-click the field in this area.

Note: To remove all the fields at once, click ◀◀ *.*

6 You can add fields from other tables by repeating steps **3** to **5** for each table.

7 Click **Next** to continue.

CONTINUED ▶

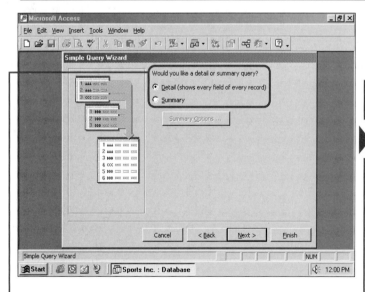

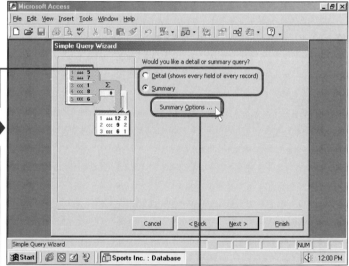

■ If your query contains information that Access can summarize, you can choose how you want to display the information in the results of your query.

*Note: If this screen does not appear, skip to step **16** on page 155 to continue creating your query.*

8 Click the way you want to display the information in the results of your query (○ changes to ⊙). If you select **Detail**, skip to step **15** on page 154.

9 Click **Summary Options** to select how you want to summarize the information.

■ The Summary Options dialog box appears.

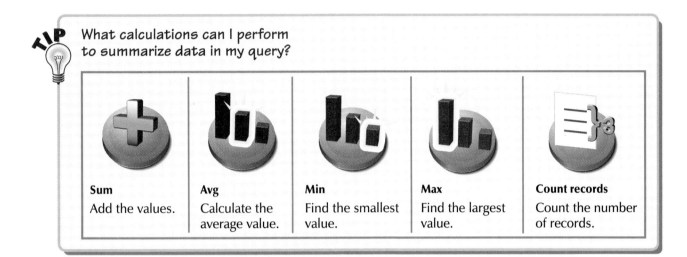

TIP

What calculations can I perform to summarize data in my query?

Sum
Add the values.

Avg
Calculate the average value.

Min
Find the smallest value.

Max
Find the largest value.

Count records
Count the number of records.

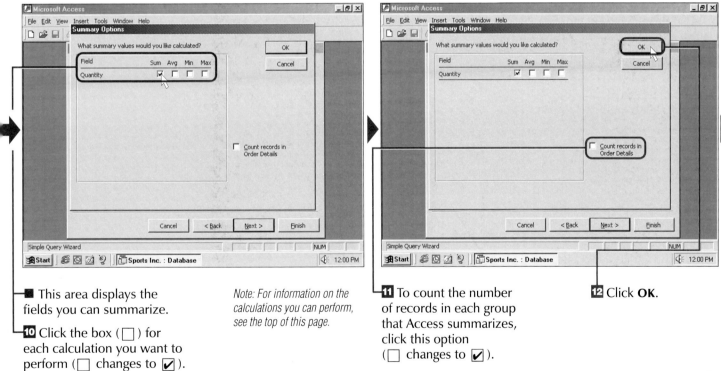

■ This area displays the fields you can summarize.

10 Click the box (□) for each calculation you want to perform (□ changes to ✔).

Note: For information on the calculations you can perform, see the top of this page.

11 To count the number of records in each group that Access summarizes, click this option (□ changes to ✔).

12 Click **OK**.

CONTINUED

If a field in your query contains dates, you can specify the way you want to group the dates.

CREATE A QUERY USING THE SIMPLE QUERY WIZARD (CONTINUED)

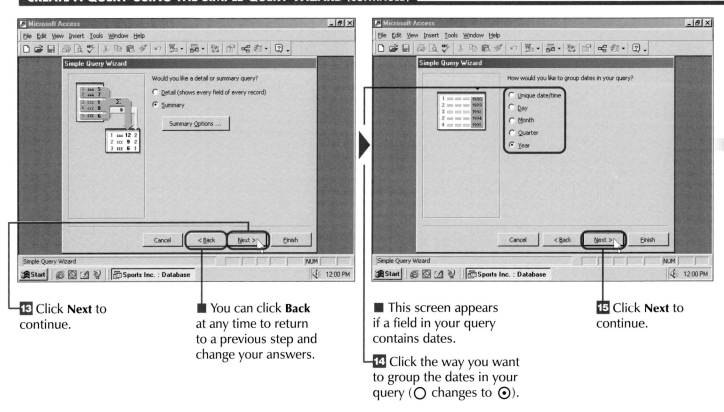

13 Click **Next** to continue.

■ You can click **Back** at any time to return to a previous step and change your answers.

■ This screen appears if a field in your query contains dates.

14 Click the way you want to group the dates in your query (○ changes to ⊙).

15 Click **Next** to continue.

Why didn't my query summarize data the way I expected?

When creating a query, make sure you only include the fields you need. For example, to determine the total number of units sold by each employee, you should only include the Employee and Units Sold fields.

Employee	Units Sold
Abbott	8,800
Carey	7,400
Davis	3,900
Jones	3,700
Lance	7,700
McMillan	8,800

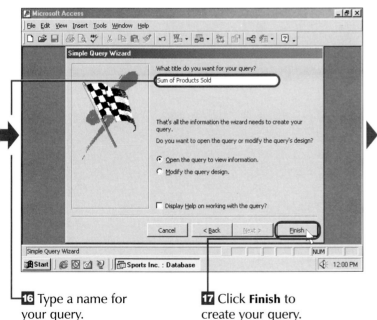

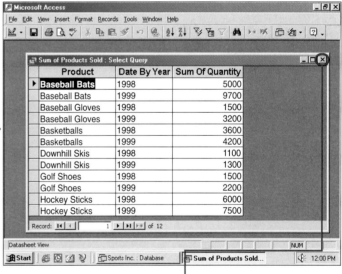

16 Type a name for your query.

17 Click **Finish** to create your query.

■ The results of your query appear.

■ When you finish viewing the results of the query, click ⊠ to close the query.

Note: You can use the Design view to make changes to your query. To display the query in the Design view, see page 156.

CHANGE VIEW OF QUERY

There are three ways you can view a query. Each view allows you to perform different tasks.

Design View   Datasheet View   SQL View

Select View

CHANGE VIEW OF QUERY

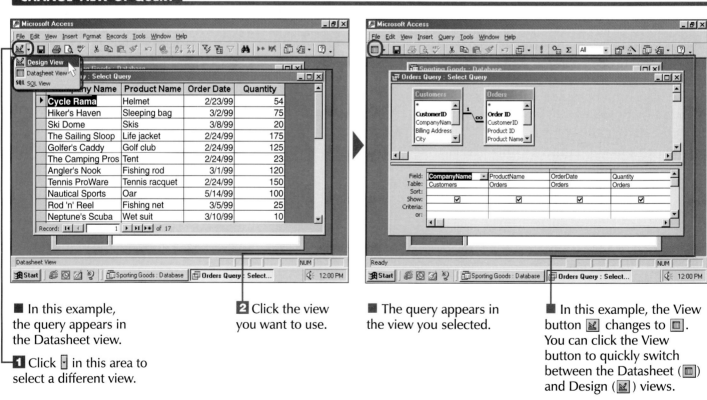

■ In this example, the query appears in the Datasheet view.

1 Click ⏷ in this area to select a different view.

2 Click the view you want to use.

■ The query appears in the view you selected.

■ In this example, the View button 🖾 changes to 🔳. You can click the View button to quickly switch between the Datasheet (🔳) and Design (🖾) views.

THE QUERY VIEWS

Design View

The Design view allows you to plan your query. You can use this view to tell Access what data you want to find, where Access can find the data and how you want to display the results.

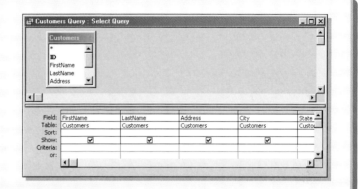

Datasheet View

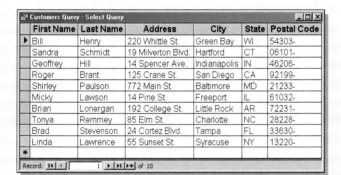

The Datasheet view displays the results of your query. The field names appear across the top of the window. Each row shows the information for one record that meets the criteria or conditions you specified.

SQL View

SQL (Structured Query Language) is a computer language. When you create a query, Access creates the SQL statements that describe your query. The SQL view displays the SQL statements for your query. You do not need to use this view to effectively use Access.

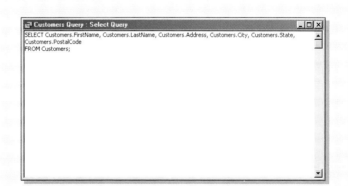

You can open a query to display the results of the query on your screen. This lets you review and make changes to the query.

Each time you open a query, Access will use the most current data from your database to determine the results of the query.

OPEN A QUERY

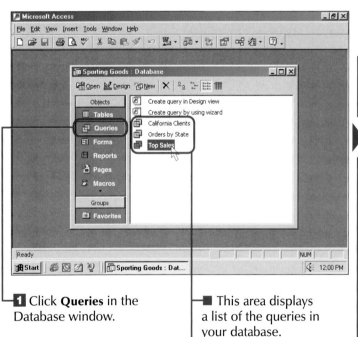

1 Click **Queries** in the Database window.

■ This area displays a list of the queries in your database.

2 Double-click the query you want to open.

■ The query opens. You can now review the results of the query.

■ When you finish working with the query, click ⊠ to close the query.

■ A dialog box will appear if you did not save changes you made to the design of the query. Click **Yes** to save the changes.

REARRANGE FIELDS

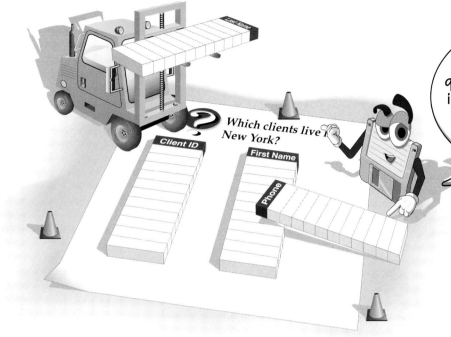

You can change the order of fields in a query. Rearranging fields in a query will affect the order that the fields appear in the query results.

REARRANGE FIELDS

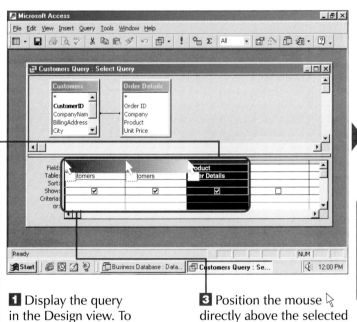

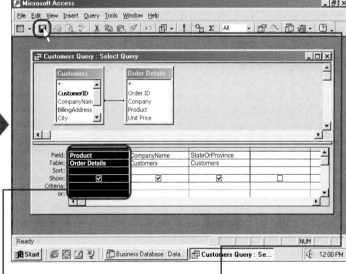

1 Display the query in the Design view. To change the view, see page 156.

2 Position the mouse ⬉ directly above the field you want to move (⬉ changes to ↓) and then click to select the field.

3 Position the mouse ⬉ directly above the selected field and then drag the field to a new location.

Note: A thick line shows where the field will appear.

■ The field appears in the new location.

4 Click 🖫 to save your change.

DELETE A FIELD

You can delete a field you no longer need from your query.

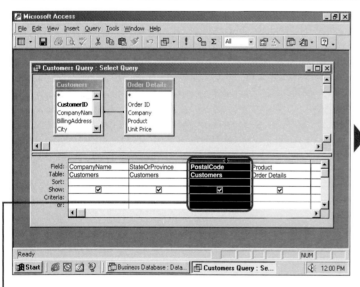

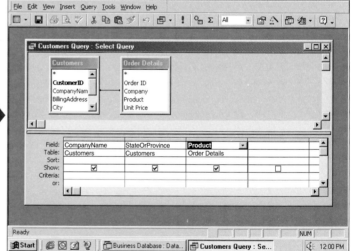

1 Position the mouse ⬚ directly above the field you want to delete (⬚ changes to ↓) and then click to select the field.

2 Press the `Delete` key.

■ The field disappears from your query.

HIDE A FIELD

You can hide a field used in a query. Hiding a field is useful when you need a field to find information in your database, but do not want the field to appear in the results of the query.

Which clients live in Florida?

Address ID	First Name	Last Name	City	State
1	Jay	Chivers	Jacksonville	Flori
2	Jody	Lee	Miami	Flori
3	Tina	Veltri	Jacksonville	Flori
4	Peter	Lejcar	Daytona Beach	Florida
5	Melanie	Robinson	Jacksonville	Florida
6	Carol	Barclay	Miami	Florida

For example, you can hide the State field if you want to find clients in Florida, but do not want the State field to appear in the query results.

HIDE A FIELD

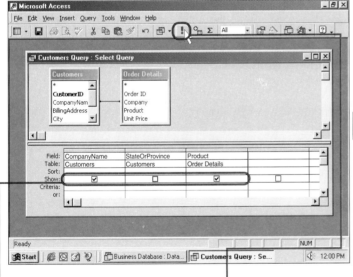

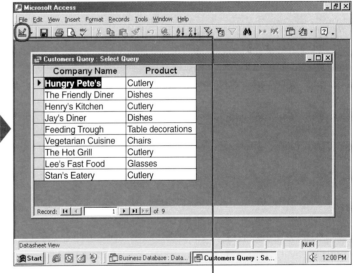

■ Each field displaying a check mark (☑) will appear in the results of the query.

1 If you do not want a field to appear in the results of the query, click the **Show** box for the field (☑ changes to ☐).

2 Click ⓘ to run the query.

■ The field does not appear in the results of the query.

■ To return to the Design view, click ⬚.

SORT QUERY RESULTS

You can sort the results of a query to better organize the results. This can help you quickly find information of interest.

There are two ways you can sort the results of a query.

Ascending
Sorts A to Z, 1 to 9

Descending
Sorts Z to A, 9 to 1

SORT QUERY RESULTS

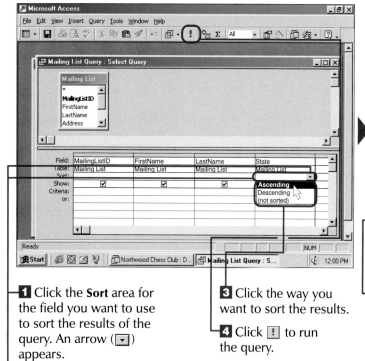

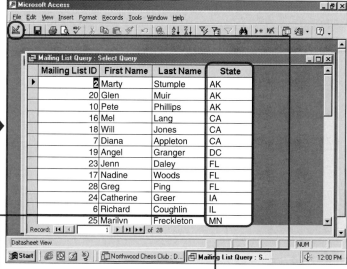

1 Click the **Sort** area for the field you want to use to sort the results of the query. An arrow (▾) appears.

2 Click the arrow (▾).

3 Click the way you want to sort the results.

4 Click ▣ to run the query.

■ The records appear in the order you specified. In this example, the records are sorted alphabetically by state.

■ To return to the Design view, click ▨ .

USING CRITERIA

You can use criteria to find specific records in your database. Criteria are conditions that identify which records you want to find.

Which customers live in California?

State = CA

Which students scored greater than 80% on their final grade?

Final grade >80%

Which recipes take less than 15 minutes to prepare?

Preparation Time <15 min

For example, you can use criteria to find customers who live in California.

USING CRITERIA

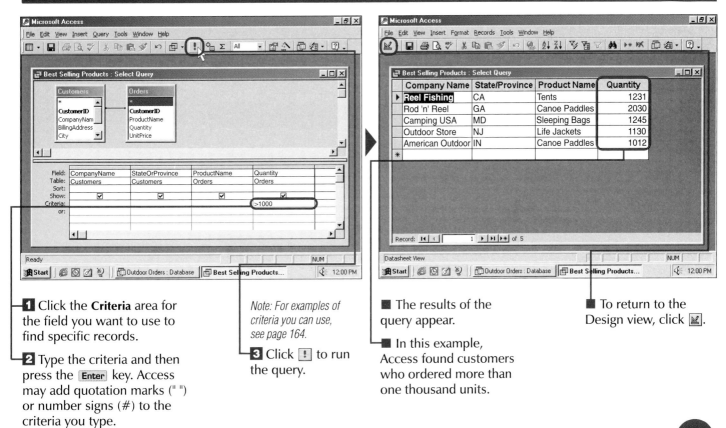

1 Click the **Criteria** area for the field you want to use to find specific records.

2 Type the criteria and then press the Enter key. Access may add quotation marks (" ") or number signs (#) to the criteria you type.

Note: For examples of criteria you can use, see page 164.

3 Click ! to run the query.

■ The results of the query appear.

■ In this example, Access found customers who ordered more than one thousand units.

■ To return to the Design view, click 🔲.

EXAMPLES OF CRITERIA

Here are examples of criteria that you can use to find records in your database. Criteria are conditions that identify the records you want to find.

Exact matches

=100	Finds the number 100.
=California	Finds the word California.
=1/5/99	Finds the date 5-Jan-99.

Note: You can leave out the equal sign (=) when searching for an exact match.

Less than

<100	Finds numbers less than 100.
<N	Finds text starting with the letters A to M.
<1/5/99	Finds dates before 5-Jan-99.

Less than or equal to

<=100	Finds numbers less than or equal to 100.
<=N	Finds the letter N and text starting with the letters A to M.
<=1/5/99	Finds dates on and before 5-Jan-99.

Greater than

>100	Finds numbers greater than 100.
>N	Finds text starting with the letters N to Z.
>1/5/99	Finds dates after 5-Jan-99.

Greater than or equal to

>=100	Finds numbers greater than or equal to 100.
>=N	Finds the letter N and text starting with the letters N to Z.
>=1/5/99	Finds dates on and after 5-Jan-99.

Not equal to

<>100
Finds numbers not equal to 100.

<>California
Finds text not equal to California.

<>1/5/99
Finds dates not on 5-Jan-99.

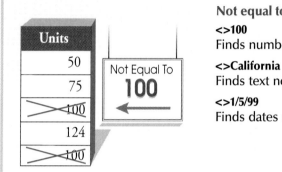

Empty fields

Is Null
Finds records that do not contain data in the field.

Is Not Null
Finds records that contain data in the field.

Find list of items

In (100,101)
Finds the numbers 100 and 101.

In (California,CA)
Finds California and CA.

In (#1/5/99#,#1/6/99#)
Finds the dates 5-Jan-99 and 6-Jan-99.

Between...And...

Between 100 And 200
Finds numbers from 100 to 200.

Between A And D
Finds the letter D and text starting with the letters A to C.

Between 1/5/99 And 1/15/99
Finds dates on and between 5-Jan-99 and 15-Jan-99.

Wildcards

The asterisk (*) wildcard represents one or more characters. The question mark (?) wildcard represents a single character.

Like Br*   Finds text starting with **Br**, such as **Br**enda and **Br**own.

Like *ar*   Finds text containing **ar**, such as **Ar**nold and M**ar**c.

Like Wend? Finds 5 letter words starting with **Wend**, such as **Wend**i and **Wend**y.

USING MULTIPLE CRITERIA

You can use multiple criteria to find records in your database. Using the "Or" condition allows you to find records that meet at least one of the criteria you specify.

Criteria are conditions that identify which records you want to find. For examples of criteria, see page 164.

USING "OR" WITH ONE FIELD

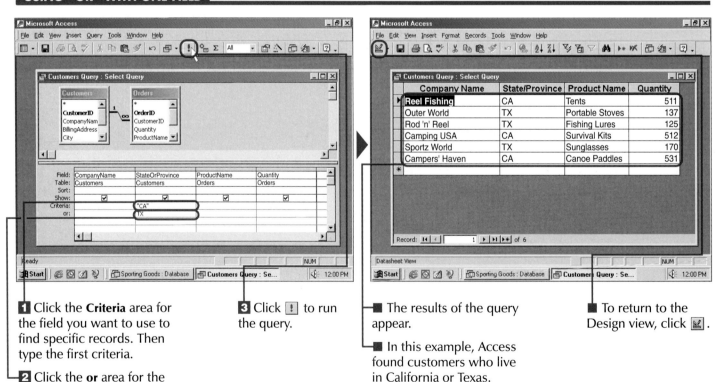

1 Click the **Criteria** area for the field you want to use to find specific records. Then type the first criteria.

2 Click the **or** area for the field you used in step **1**. Then type the second criteria.

3 Click ! to run the query.

■ The results of the query appear.

■ In this example, Access found customers who live in California or Texas.

■ To return to the Design view, click 🔍.

166

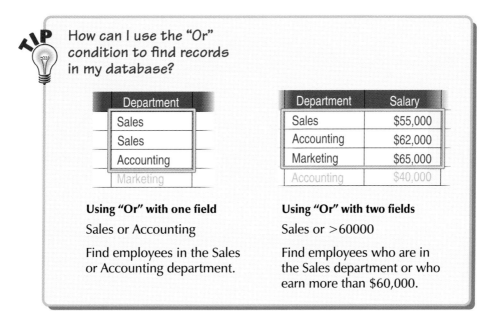

How can I use the "Or" condition to find records in my database?

Department
Sales
Sales
Accounting
Marketing

Department	Salary
Sales	$55,000
Accounting	$62,000
Marketing	$65,000
Accounting	$40,000

Using "Or" with one field

Sales or Accounting

Find employees in the Sales or Accounting department.

Using "Or" with two fields

Sales or >60000

Find employees who are in the Sales department or who earn more than $60,000.

USING "OR" WITH TWO FIELDS

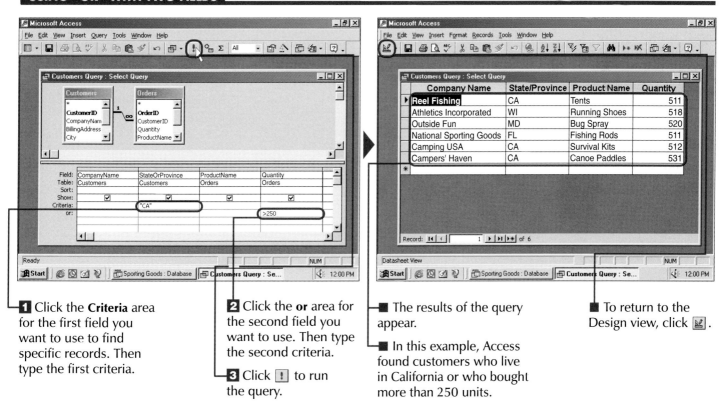

1 Click the **Criteria** area for the first field you want to use to find specific records. Then type the first criteria.

2 Click the **or** area for the second field you want to use. Then type the second criteria.

3 Click [!] to run the query.

■ The results of the query appear.

■ In this example, Access found customers who live in California or who bought more than 250 units.

■ To return to the Design view, click 🔛.

USING MULTIPLE CRITERIA

You can use multiple criteria to find records in your database. Using the "And" condition allows you to find records that meet all of the criteria you specify.

Recipe ID	Recipe Name	Calories/Serving	Vegetarian
1	Chicken Stir-fry	180	No
2	Omelet	200	Yes
3	Veggie		
4	Lasag		
5	Panca		

Find: Vegetarian
And
Under 225 Calories

Recipe ID	Recipe Name	Calories/Serving	Vegetarian
2	Omelet	200	Yes
3	Veggie Pizza	215	Yes
5	Pancakes	180	Yes

Criteria are conditions that identify which records you want to find. For examples of criteria, see page 164.

USING "AND" WITH ONE FIELD

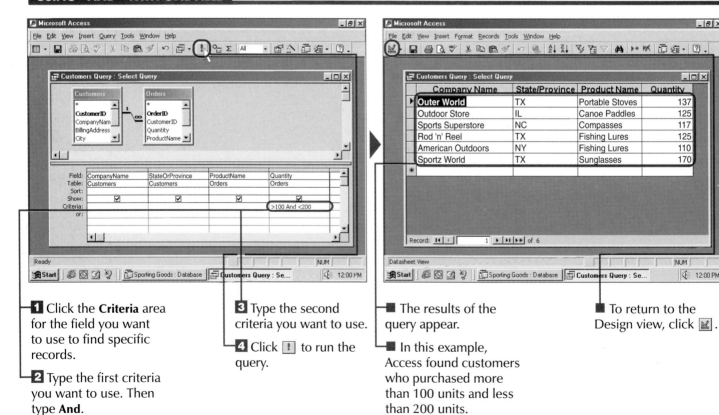

1 Click the **Criteria** area for the field you want to use to find specific records.

2 Type the first criteria you want to use. Then type **And**.

3 Type the second criteria you want to use.

4 Click [!] to run the query.

■ The results of the query appear.

■ In this example, Access found customers who purchased more than 100 units and less than 200 units.

■ To return to the Design view, click [ ].

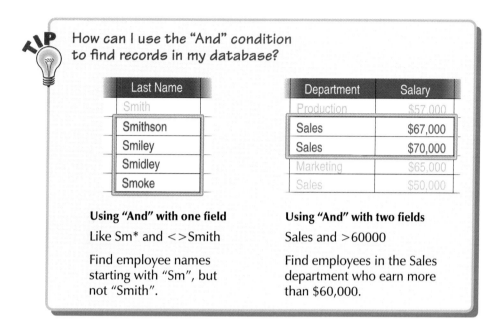

TIP

How can I use the "And" condition to find records in my database?

Last Name
Smith
Smithson
Smiley
Smidley
Smoke

Department	Salary
Production	$57,000
Sales	$67,000
Sales	$70,000
Marketing	$65,000
Sales	$50,000

Using "And" with one field

Like Sm* and <>Smith

Find employee names starting with "Sm", but not "Smith".

Using "And" with two fields

Sales and >60000

Find employees in the Sales department who earn more than $60,000.

USING "AND" WITH TWO FIELDS

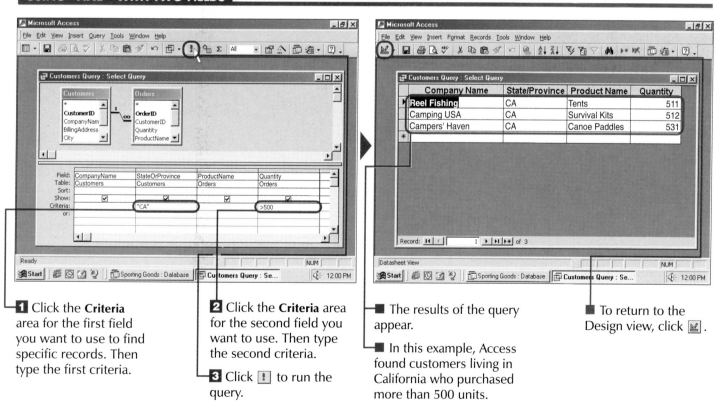

1 Click the **Criteria** area for the first field you want to use to find specific records. Then type the first criteria.

2 Click the **Criteria** area for the second field you want to use. Then type the second criteria.

3 Click !️ to run the query.

■ The results of the query appear.

■ In this example, Access found customers living in California who purchased more than 500 units.

■ To return to the Design view, click ⊞ .

PERFORM CALCULATIONS

You can perform calculations on each record in your database. You can then review and analyze the results.

Job ID	Rate/Hr	Hours	Total
1	$17.00 X	8 =	$136.00
2	$25.00	11.5	$287.50
3	$20.00	18.2	$364.0
4	$30.00	4	$120
5	$60.00	27.5	$

You can use these operators to perform calculations.

+ Add

- Subtract

* Multiply

/ Divide

^ Raise to a power

PERFORM CALCULATIONS

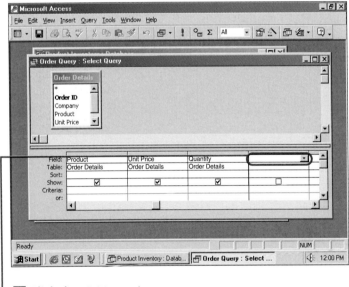

1 Click the **Field** area in the first empty column.

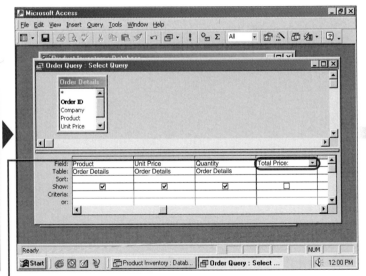

2 Type a name for the field that will display the results of the calculations, followed by a colon (:). Then press the **Spacebar** to leave a blank space.

How do I enter an expression to perform a calculation?

[Orders]![Quantity]*[Orders]![Price]

To enter a field in an expression, type the name of the table containing the field in square brackets (**[Orders]**) followed by an exclamation mark (**!**). Then type the field name in square brackets (**[Quantity]**). Make sure you type the table and field names exactly.

[Quantity]*[Price]

If a field exists in only one table, you do not need to enter the table name.

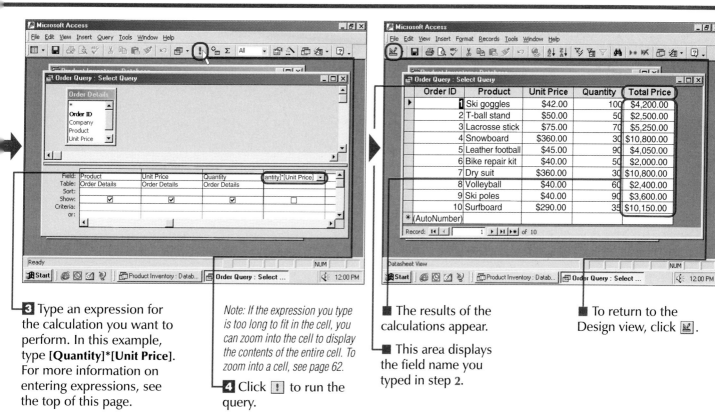

3 Type an expression for the calculation you want to perform. In this example, type **[Quantity]*[Unit Price]**. For more information on entering expressions, see the top of this page.

Note: If the expression you type is too long to fit in the cell, you can zoom into the cell to display the contents of the entire cell. To zoom into a cell, see page 62.

4 Click [!] to run the query.

■ The results of the calculations appear.

■ This area displays the field name you typed in step **2**.

■ To return to the Design view, click [≌].

SUMMARIZE DATA

COMPANY	QTY ORDERED
Wild Adventures	40
Sports Inc.	60
Racquets Plus	70
Ski World	30
Bike Time Inc.	25
The Ski Club	60
Mountain Top	90
Time	30

You can summarize the data in a field to help you analyze the data.

For example, you can summarize data in the Quantity Ordered field to determine the total amount of products ordered.

SUMMARIZE DATA FOR ONE FIELD

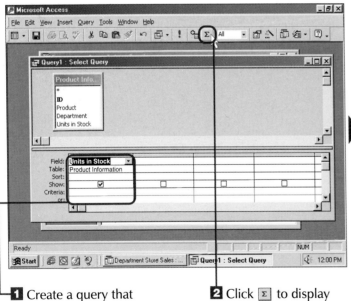

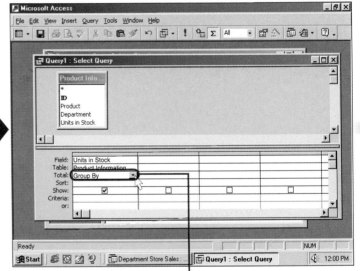

1 Create a query that includes only the field you want to summarize. To create a query in the Design view, see page 146.

2 Click ∑ to display the Total row.

■ The Total row appears.

Note: You can repeat step 2 at any time to remove the Total row.

3 Click the **Total** area for the field. An arrow (▼) appears.

4 Click the arrow (▼) to display a list of calculations you can perform.

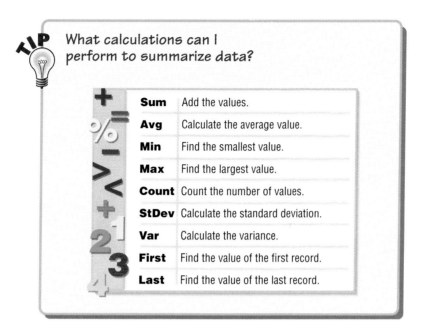

TIP

What calculations can I perform to summarize data?

Sum	Add the values.
Avg	Calculate the average value.
Min	Find the smallest value.
Max	Find the largest value.
Count	Count the number of values.
StDev	Calculate the standard deviation.
Var	Calculate the variance.
First	Find the value of the first record.
Last	Find the value of the last record.

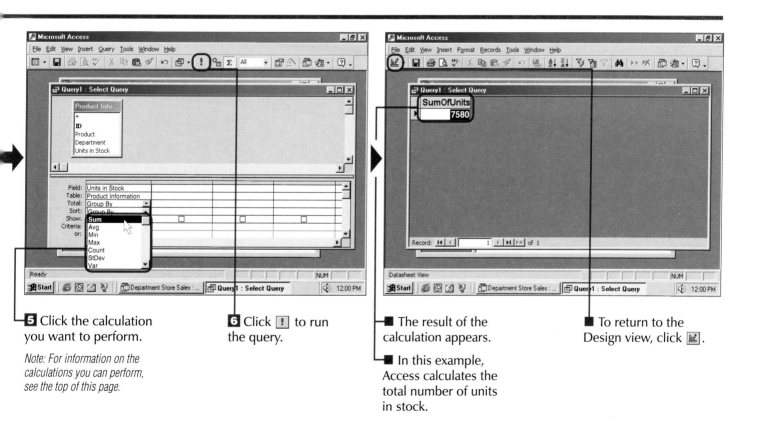

5 Click the calculation you want to perform.

Note: For information on the calculations you can perform, see the top of this page.

6 Click ▮ to run the query.

■ The result of the calculation appears.

■ In this example, Access calculates the total number of units in stock.

■ To return to the Design view, click ▨.

You can group records in your database and summarize the data for each group.

For example, you can group records by date and determine the total number of orders for each day.

SUMMARIZE DATA FOR GROUPED RECORDS

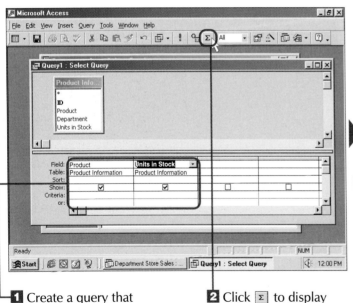

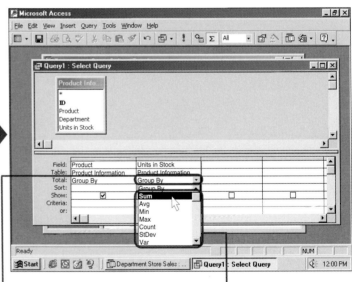

1 Create a query that includes only the field you want to use to group your records and the field you want to summarize. To create a query in the Design view, see page 146.

2 Click ∑ to display the Total row.

■ The Total row appears.

Note: You can repeat step 2 at any time to remove the Total row.

3 Click the **Total** area for the field you want to summarize. An arrow (▼) appears.

4 Click the arrow (▼) to display a list of calculations you can perform.

5 Click the calculation you want to perform.

Note: For information on the calculations you can perform, see the top of page 173.

Can I use more than one field to group records?

You can group records using more than one field. For example, to determine the total amount of each product purchased by each company, use the Company and Product fields to group records and the Quantity Ordered field to summarize data.

COMPANY	PRODUCT	QUANTITY ORDERED
Fitness Minds	A	40
Fitness Minds	B	60
Racquets Plus	A	80
Racquets Plus	B	30
Ski World	A	25
Ski World	B	60
SportStop	A	90
SportStop	B	100

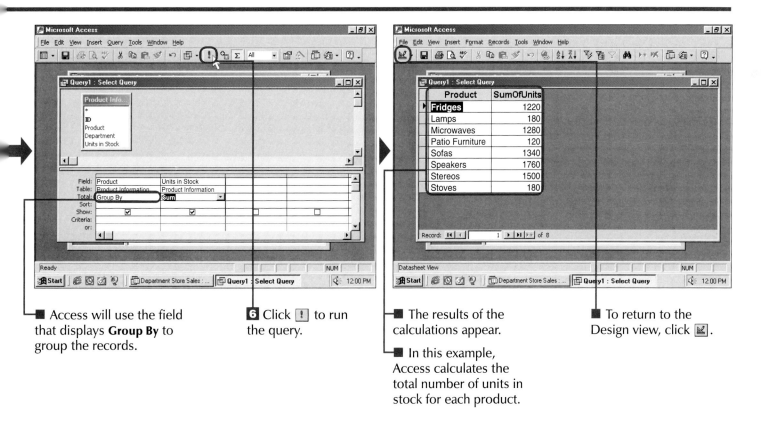

■ Access will use the field that displays **Group By** to group the records.

6 Click ！ to run the query.

■ The results of the calculations appear.

■ In this example, Access calculates the total number of units in stock for each product.

■ To return to the Design view, click 🖉.

First Quarter Sales

Product	Baseball Bats		Unit Price
	Month	**Quantity Sold**	
	January	3200	$29.99
	February	3000	$29.99
	March	2000	$29.99

Summary for 'Product' = Baseball Bats (3 detail records)

Sum 8200

Product	Baseball Gloves		Unit Price
	Month	**Quantity Sold**	
	January	3200	$39.99

CHAPTER 10

CREATE REPORTS

Would you like to present your data in a professional-looking report? This chapter teaches you how to create and work with reports.

You can use the Report Wizard to create a professionally designed report that summarizes data in your database.

The Report Wizard asks you a series of questions and then creates a report based on your answers.

CREATE A REPORT USING THE REPORT WIZARD

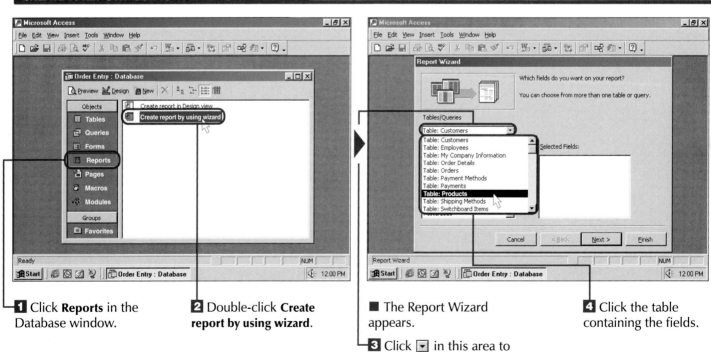

1 Click **Reports** in the Database window.

2 Double-click **Create report by using wizard**.

■ The Report Wizard appears.

3 Click ▼ in this area to select the table containing the fields you want to include in your report.

4 Click the table containing the fields.

Which tables in my database can I use to create a report?

You can use any table in your database to create a report. To create a report using data from more than one table, relationships must exist between the tables. For information on relationships, see page 104.

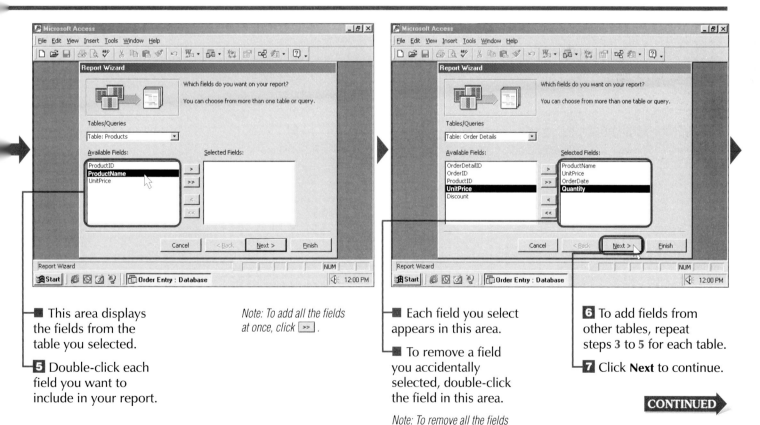

■ This area displays the fields from the table you selected.

5 Double-click each field you want to include in your report.

Note: To add all the fields at once, click 📧 *.*

■ Each field you select appears in this area.

■ To remove a field you accidentally selected, double-click the field in this area.

Note: To remove all the fields at once, click 📧 *.*

6 To add fields from other tables, repeat steps **3** to **5** for each table.

7 Click **Next** to continue.

CONTINUED

You can choose how you want to group data in your report. Grouping data helps you organize and summarize the data in your report.

For example, you can group all the customers from the same state together in your report.

CREATE A REPORT USING THE REPORT WIZARD (CONTINUED)

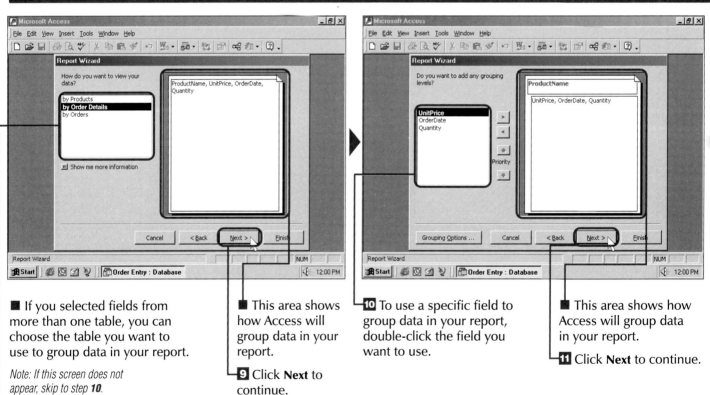

■ If you selected fields from more than one table, you can choose the table you want to use to group data in your report.

Note: If this screen does not appear, skip to step 10.

8 Click the table you want to use to group data in your report.

■ This area shows how Access will group data in your report.

9 Click **Next** to continue.

10 To use a specific field to group data in your report, double-click the field you want to use.

■ This area shows how Access will group data in your report.

11 Click **Next** to continue.

Why would I sort the records in my report?

You can sort the records in your report to better organize the data. For example, you can alphabetically sort records by the Last Name field to make it easier to find customers of interest. If the same last name appears more than once in the field, you can sort by a second field, such as First Name.

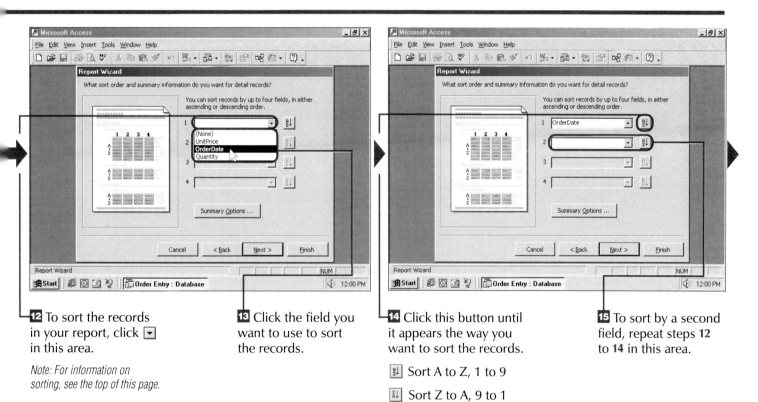

12 To sort the records in your report, click ▾ in this area.

Note: For information on sorting, see the top of this page.

13 Click the field you want to use to sort the records.

14 Click this button until it appears the way you want to sort the records.

▯↓ Sort A to Z, 1 to 9

▯↓ Sort Z to A, 9 to 1

15 To sort by a second field, repeat steps **12** to **14** in this area.

CONTINUED

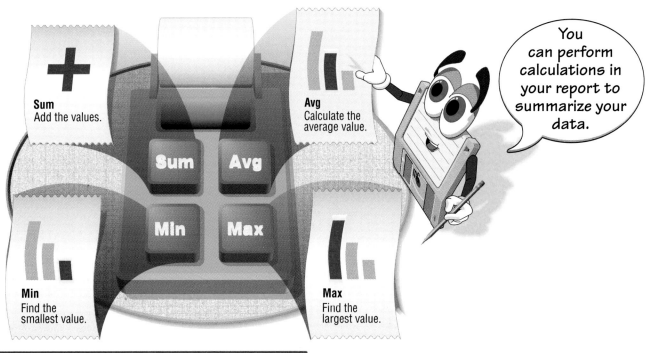

Sum
Add the values.

Avg
Calculate the average value.

Min
Find the smallest value.

Max
Find the largest value.

You can perform calculations in your report to summarize your data.

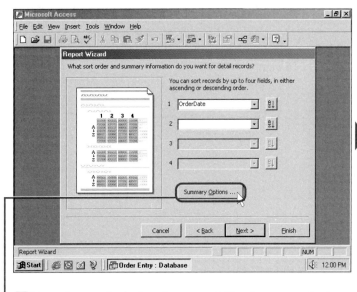

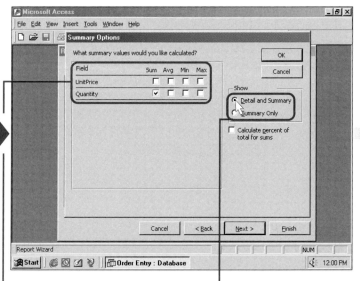

16 To perform calculations in your report, click **Summary Options**.

*Note: Summary Options may not be available for some reports. If Summary Options is not available, skip to step **21** to continue creating the report.*

■ The Summary Options dialog box appears.

■ This area displays the fields you can perform calculations on.

17 Click the box (☐) for each calculation you want to perform (☐ changes to ☑).

18 Click an option to specify if you want to display all the records and the summary or just the summary (○ changes to ◉). For more information, see the top of page 183.

182

When performing calculations in my report, what information can I include?

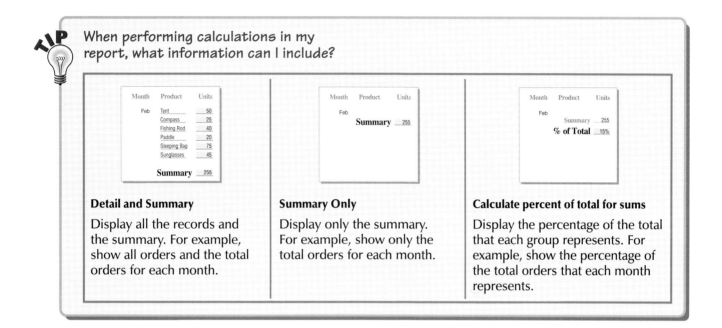

Detail and Summary

Display all the records and the summary. For example, show all orders and the total orders for each month.

Summary Only

Display only the summary. For example, show only the total orders for each month.

Calculate percent of total for sums

Display the percentage of the total that each group represents. For example, show the percentage of the total orders that each month represents.

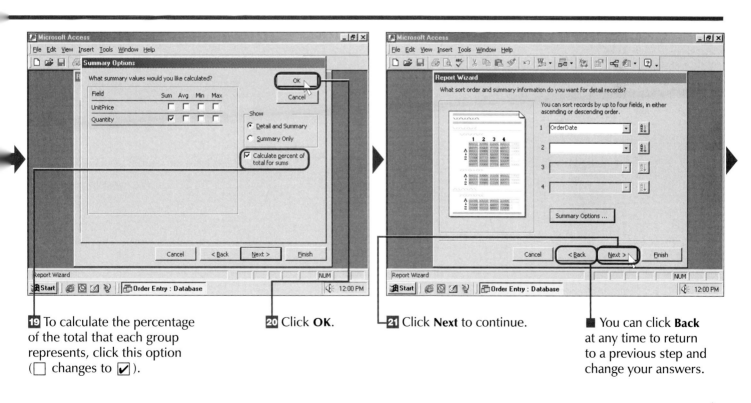

19 To calculate the percentage of the total that each group represents, click this option (☐ changes to ☑).

20 Click **OK**.

21 Click **Next** to continue.

■ You can click **Back** at any time to return to a previous step and change your answers.

CONTINUED

You can choose from several layouts for your report. The layout determines the arrangement of information in your report.

CREATE A REPORT USING THE REPORT WIZARD (CONTINUED)

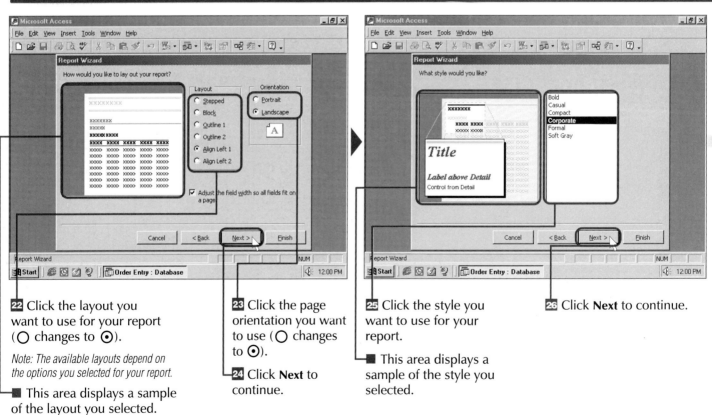

22 Click the layout you want to use for your report (○ changes to ⊙).

Note: The available layouts depend on the options you selected for your report.

■ This area displays a sample of the layout you selected.

23 Click the page orientation you want to use (○ changes to ⊙).

24 Click **Next** to continue.

25 Click the style you want to use for your report.

■ This area displays a sample of the style you selected.

26 Click **Next** to continue.

Do I need to create a new report each time I change the data in my database?

No. Each time you open a report, Access gathers the most current data from your database to create the report. This ensures that the report always displays the most up-to-date information.

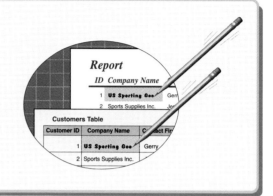

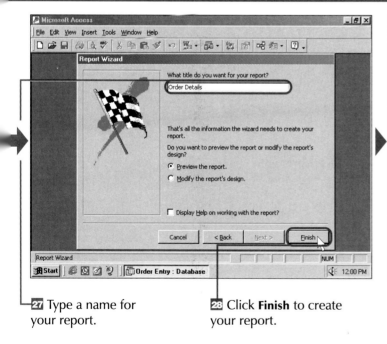

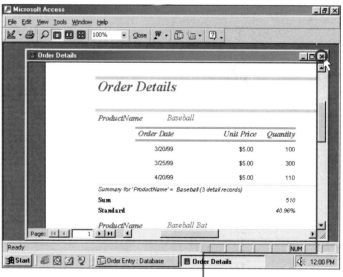

27 Type a name for your report.

28 Click **Finish** to create your report.

■ A window appears, displaying your report.

Note: To move through the pages in a report, see page 190.

29 When you finish viewing the report, click ☒ to close the report.

You can use the AutoReport Wizard to quickly create a report that displays the information from a table in your database.

Columnar AutoReport

Displays records in a column.

Tabular AutoReport

Displays records in rows.

CREATE A REPORT USING AN AUTOREPORT

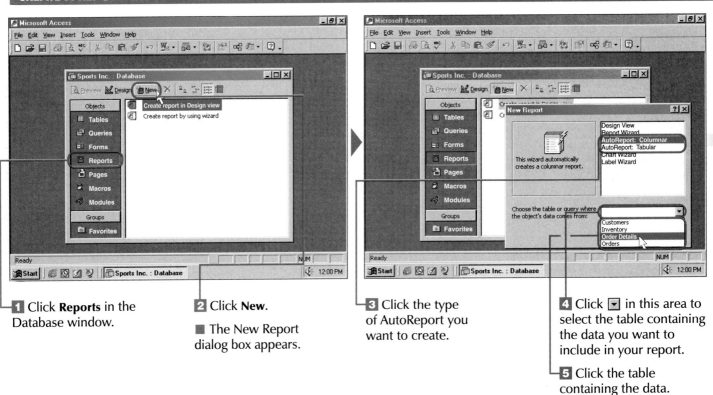

1 Click **Reports** in the Database window.

2 Click **New**.

■ The New Report dialog box appears.

3 Click the type of AutoReport you want to create.

4 Click ▾ in this area to select the table containing the data you want to include in your report.

5 Click the table containing the data.

Can I change the data displayed in a report?

If you want to make changes to the data displayed in a report, you must change the data in the table you used to create the report. Changes you make to data in the table will automatically appear in the report the next time you open the report.

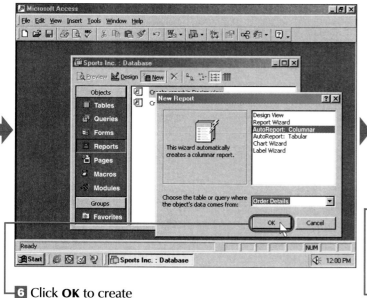

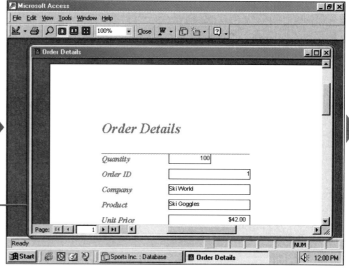

6 Click **OK** to create your report.

■ A window appears, displaying your report.

■ To move through the pages of a report, see page 190.

CONTINUED

After you create a report using the AutoReport Wizard, you need to save the report to store it for future use.

CREATE A REPORT USING AN AUTOREPORT (CONTINUED)

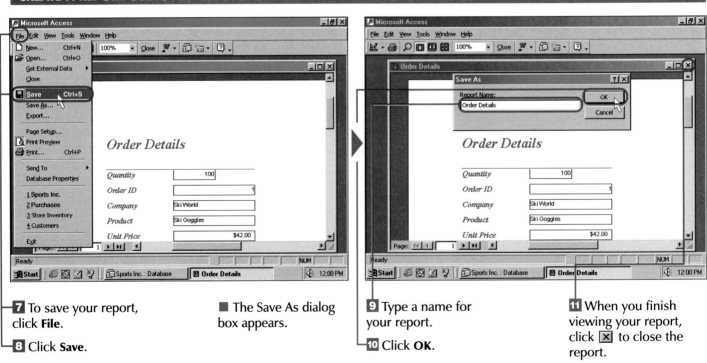

7 To save your report, click **File**.

8 Click **Save**.

■ The Save As dialog box appears.

9 Type a name for your report.

10 Click **OK**.

11 When you finish viewing your report, click ☒ to close the report.

OPEN A REPORT

You can open a report to display the contents of the report on your screen.

Each time you open a report, Access gathers the most current data from your database to create the report.

OPEN A REPORT

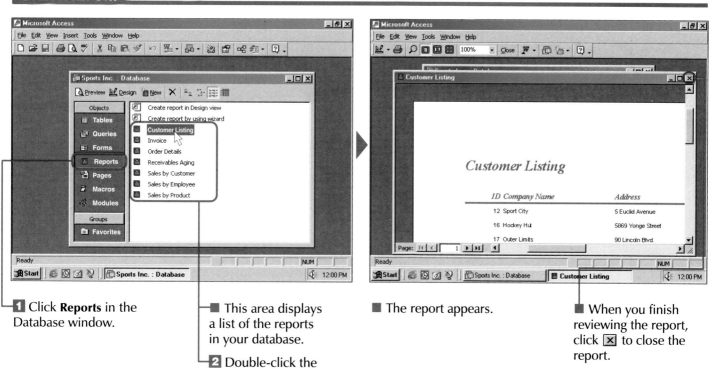

1 Click **Reports** in the Database window.

■ This area displays a list of the reports in your database.

2 Double-click the report you want to open.

■ The report appears.

■ When you finish reviewing the report, click ☒ to close the report.

If your report contains more than one page, you can move through the pages to review the information.

MOVE THROUGH PAGES

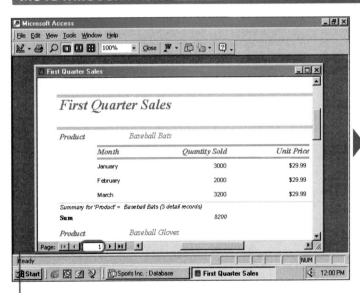

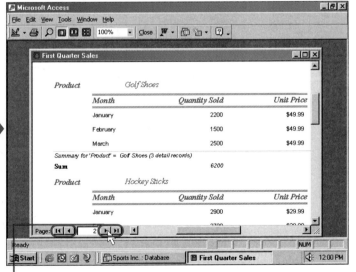

◼ This area shows the number of the page displayed on your screen.

1 If your report contains more than one page, click one of these buttons to display another page.

Note: If a button is dimmed, the button is currently not available.

⏮ First page

◀ Previous page

▶ Next page

⏭ Last page

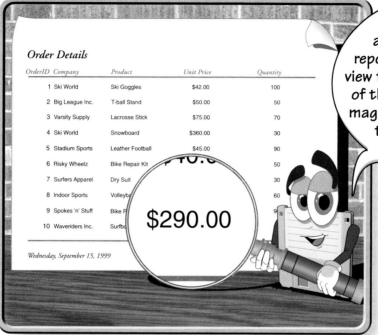

You can display an entire page of a report on your screen to view the overall appearance of the page. You can also magnify an area of a page to view the area in more detail.

ZOOM IN OR OUT

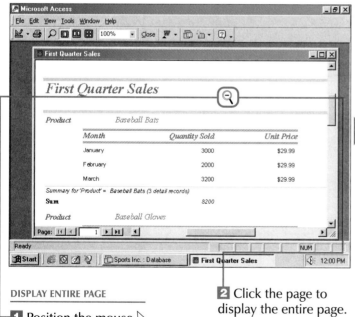

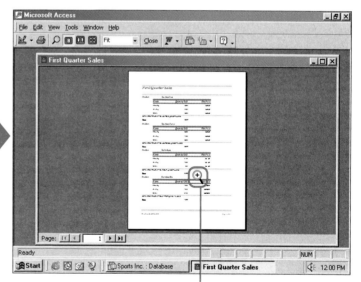

DISPLAY ENTIRE PAGE

1 Position the mouse ⤢ anywhere over the page (⤢ changes to ⊖).

2 Click the page to display the entire page.

■ The entire page appears.

MAGNIFY AREA OF PAGE

1 Position the mouse ⤢ over the area of the page you want to magnify (⤢ changes to ⊕).

2 Click the area to magnify the area.

There are three ways you can view a report. Each view allows you to perform different tasks.

- ☐ Design View
- ☐ Print Preview View
- ☑ Layout Preview View

CHANGE VIEW OF REPORT

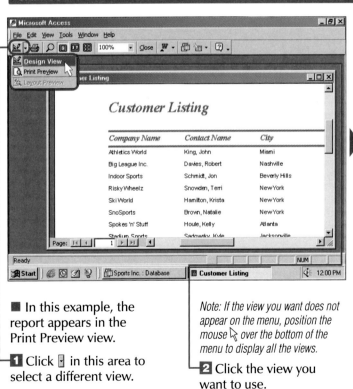

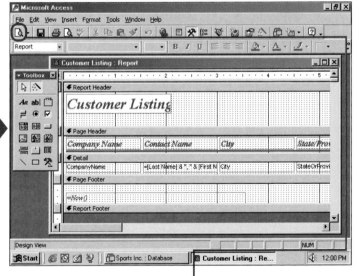

■ In this example, the report appears in the Print Preview view.

1 Click ⬝ in this area to select a different view.

Note: If the view you want does not appear on the menu, position the mouse ⬝ over the bottom of the menu to display all the views.

2 Click the view you want to use.

Note: The available views depend on the view you are currently using.

■ The report appears in the view you selected.

■ In this example, the View button 🖾 changes to 🔍. You can click the View button to quickly switch between the Print Preview (🔍) and Design (🖾) views.

192

THE REPORT VIEWS

Design View

The Design view allows you to change the layout and design of a report. This view displays small, evenly spaced dots to help you line up the items in a report. Information in this view appears in several sections, such as the Report Header and Page Footer sections.

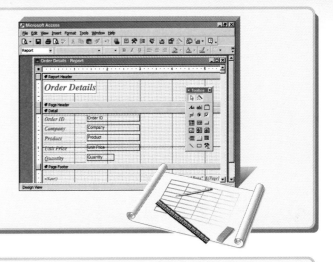

Print Preview View

The Print Preview view allows you to see how a report will look when printed. You can use this view to move through the pages in a report and examine how each page will print.

Layout Preview View

The Layout Preview view allows you to quickly view the layout and style of a report. This view is similar to the Print Preview view, but may not display all the data in the report.

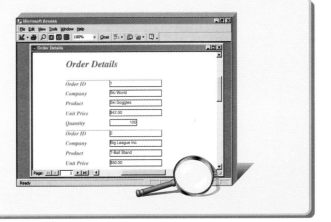

CHAPTER 11

PRINT INFORMATION

Are you wondering how to produce a paper copy of information in your database? This chapter teaches you how.

You can use the Print Preview feature to see how a table, query, form or report will look when printed. This lets you confirm that the printed pages will appear the way you want.

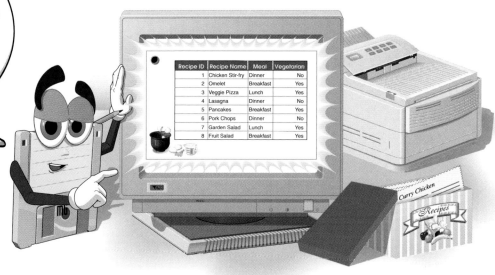

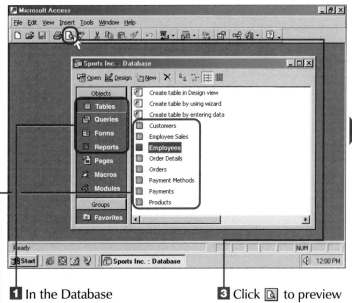

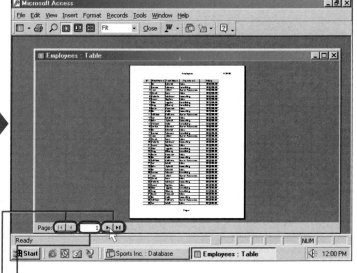

1 In the Database window, click the type of object you want to preview.

2 Click the object you want to preview.

3 Click to preview the object.

■ The Print Preview window appears, displaying the object as it will look when printed.

■ This area shows the number of the page displayed on your screen.

4 If the object contains more than one page, click one of these buttons to display another page.

First page

Previous page

Next page

Last page

Note: If a button is dimmed, the button is currently not available.

196

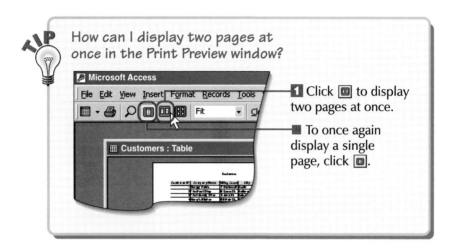

TIP

How can I display two pages at once in the Print Preview window?

1 Click 🔳 to display two pages at once.

■ To once again display a single page, click 🔳.

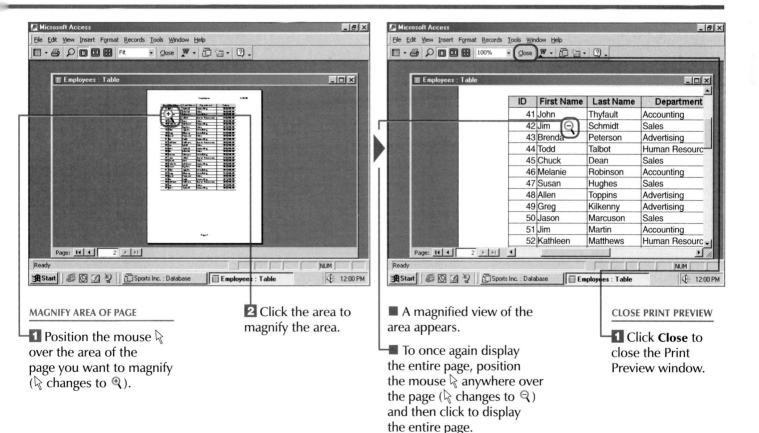

MAGNIFY AREA OF PAGE

1 Position the mouse ⌖ over the area of the page you want to magnify (⌖ changes to ⊕).

2 Click the area to magnify the area.

■ A magnified view of the area appears.

■ To once again display the entire page, position the mouse ⌖ anywhere over the page (⌖ changes to ⊖) and then click to display the entire page.

CLOSE PRINT PREVIEW

1 Click **Close** to close the Print Preview window.

You can change the way information appears on a printed page.

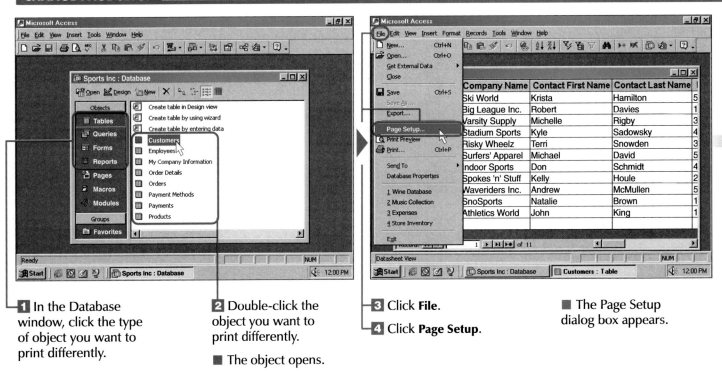

1 In the Database window, click the type of object you want to print differently.

2 Double-click the object you want to print differently.

■ The object opens.

3 Click **File**.

4 Click **Page Setup**.

■ The Page Setup dialog box appears.

198

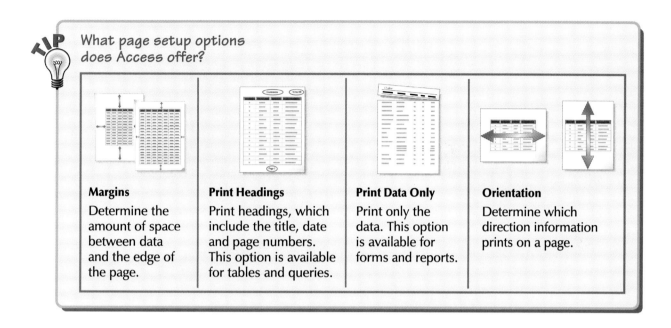

TIP What page setup options does Access offer?

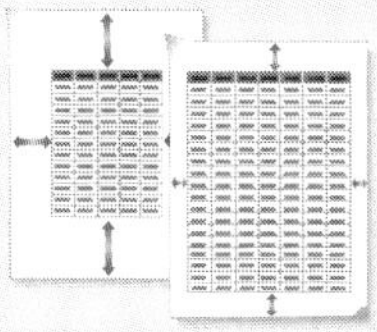

Margins

Determine the amount of space between data and the edge of the page.

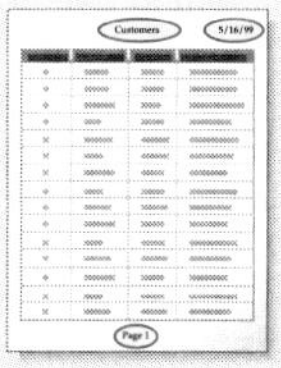

Print Headings

Print headings, which include the title, date and page numbers. This option is available for tables and queries.

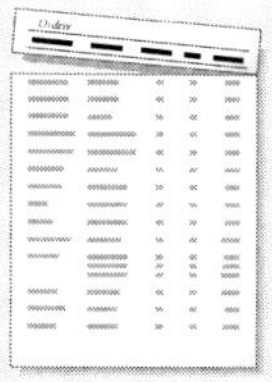

Print Data Only

Print only the data. This option is available for forms and reports.

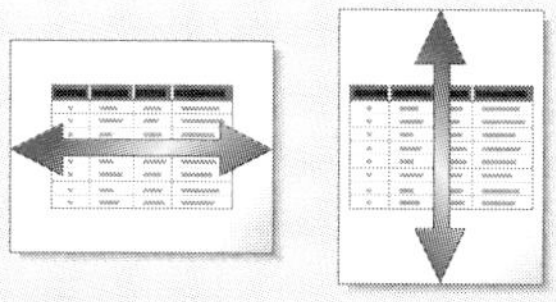

Orientation

Determine which direction information prints on a page.

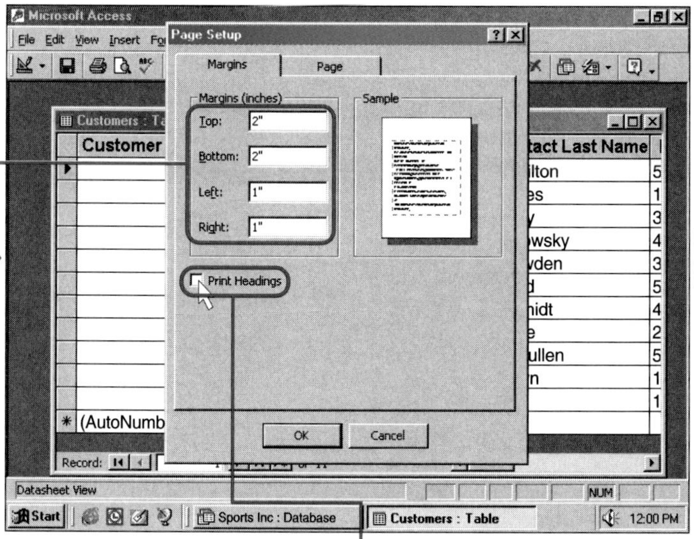

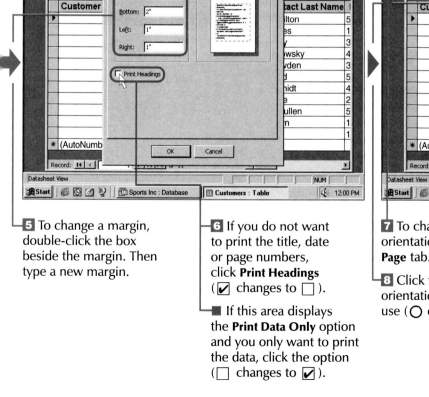

5 To change a margin, double-click the box beside the margin. Then type a new margin.

6 If you do not want to print the title, date or page numbers, click **Print Headings** (☑ changes to ☐).

■ If this area displays the **Print Data Only** option and you only want to print the data, click the option (☐ changes to ☑).

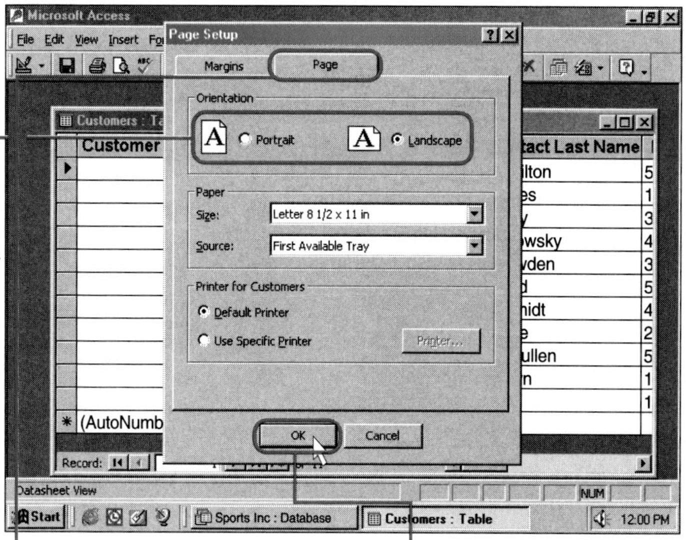

7 To change the page orientation, click the **Page** tab.

8 Click the page orientation you want to use (○ changes to ⊙).

9 Click **OK** to confirm your changes.

Note: You can use the Print Preview feature to preview the changes you made. To use the Print Preview feature, see page 196.

You can produce a paper copy of a table, query, form or report.

When you print a table or query, Access prints the title, date and page number on each page.

PRINT INFORMATION

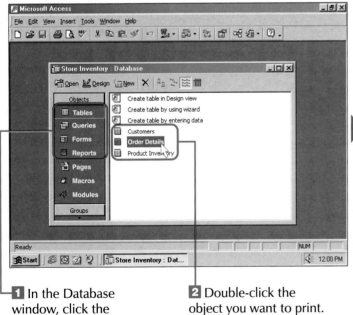

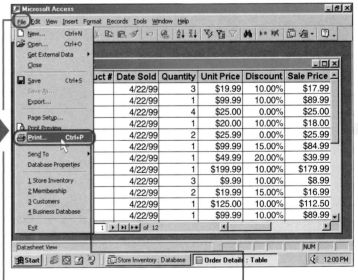

1 In the Database window, click the type of object you want to print.

2 Double-click the object you want to print.

■ The object opens.

■ If more than one record appears on your screen and you only want to print a few records, select the records you want to print. To select records, see page 54.

3 Click **File**.

4 Click **Print**.

■ The Print dialog box appears.

200

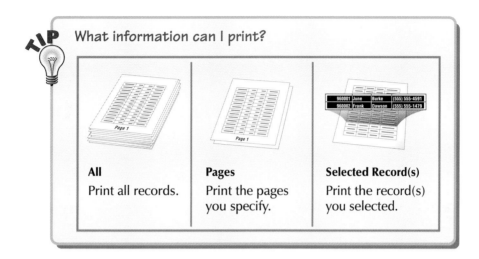

What information can I print?

All
Print all records.

Pages
Print the pages you specify.

Selected Record(s)
Print the record(s) you selected.

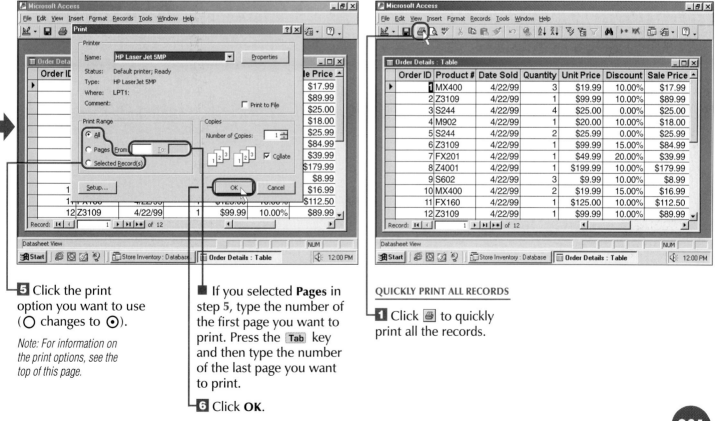

5 Click the print option you want to use (○ changes to ⊙).

Note: For information on the print options, see the top of this page.

■ If you selected **Pages** in step 5, type the number of the first page you want to print. Press the `Tab` key and then type the number of the last page you want to print.

6 Click **OK**.

QUICKLY PRINT ALL RECORDS

1 Click 🖨 to quickly print all the records.

201

CHAPTER 12

ACCESS AND THE INTERNET

Would you like to use Access to share information with other people on the Internet? Learn how in this chapter.

You can use the Page Wizard to create a data access page. A data access page is a Web page that allows you to view and edit data in your database from the Internet or your company's intranet.

An intranet is a small version of the Internet within a company.

To create a data access page, you must have Internet Explorer 5 or a later version installed on your computer.

CREATE A DATA ACCESS PAGE

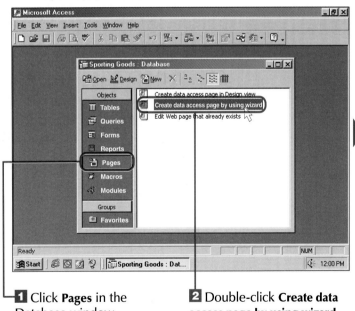

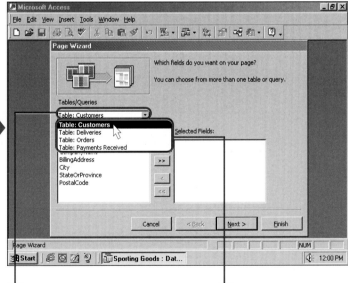

1 Click **Pages** in the Database window.

2 Double-click **Create data access page by using wizard**.

■ The Page Wizard appears.

3 Click ▾ in this area to select the table containing the fields you want to include in your page.

4 Click the table containing the fields.

Which tables in my database can I use to create a data access page?

You can use any table in your database to create a data access page. To create a data access page using data from more than one table, relationships must exist between the tables. For information on relationships, see page 104.

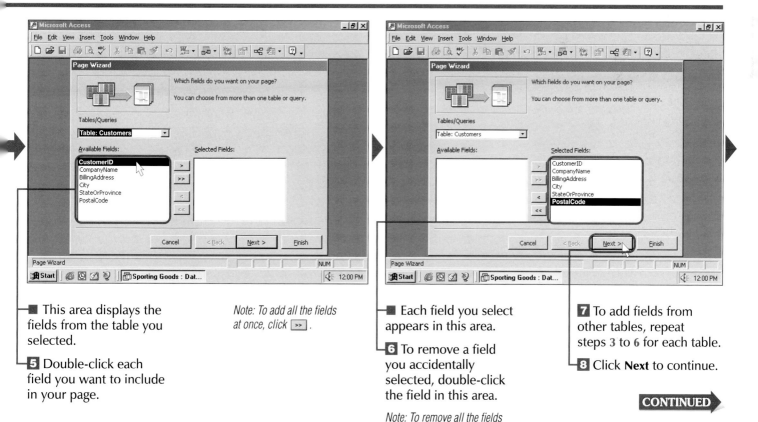

■ This area displays the fields from the table you selected.

5 Double-click each field you want to include in your page.

Note: To add all the fields at once, click >> .

■ Each field you select appears in this area.

6 To remove a field you accidentally selected, double-click the field in this area.

Note: To remove all the fields at once, click << .

7 To add fields from other tables, repeat steps **3** to **6** for each table.

8 Click **Next** to continue.

CONTINUED

> You can group data in your data access page. Grouping data helps you organize the data in your page.

For example, you can group all the customers from the same state together in your page.

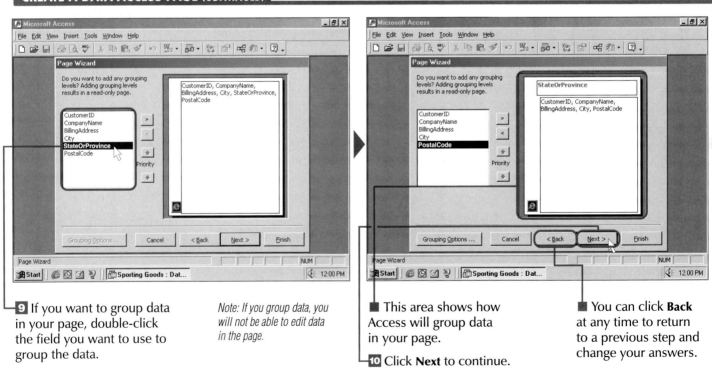

9 If you want to group data in your page, double-click the field you want to use to group the data.

Note: If you group data, you will not be able to edit data in the page.

■ This area shows how Access will group data in your page.

10 Click **Next** to continue.

■ You can click **Back** at any time to return to a previous step and change your answers.

Why would I sort the records in my page?

You can sort the records in your page to better organize the data. For example, you can sort records alphabetically by the Last Name field to make it easier to find customers of interest. If the same last name appears more than once in the field, you can sort by a second field, such as First Name, to further organize the data.

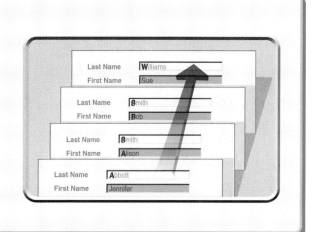

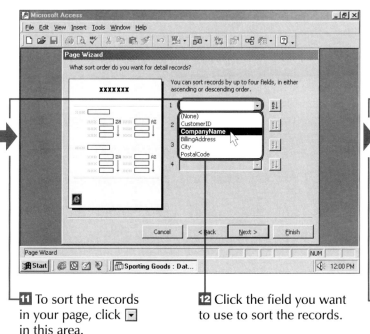

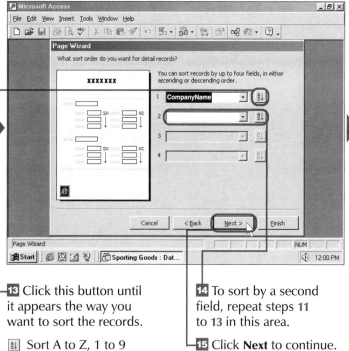

11 To sort the records in your page, click ▾ in this area.

Note: For information on sorting, see the top of this page.

12 Click the field you want to use to sort the records.

13 Click this button until it appears the way you want to sort the records.

⬆ Sort A to Z, 1 to 9

⬇ Sort Z to A, 9 to 1

14 To sort by a second field, repeat steps **11** to **13** in this area.

15 Click **Next** to continue.

CONTINUED ▶

When creating a data access page, you can give the page a descriptive title.

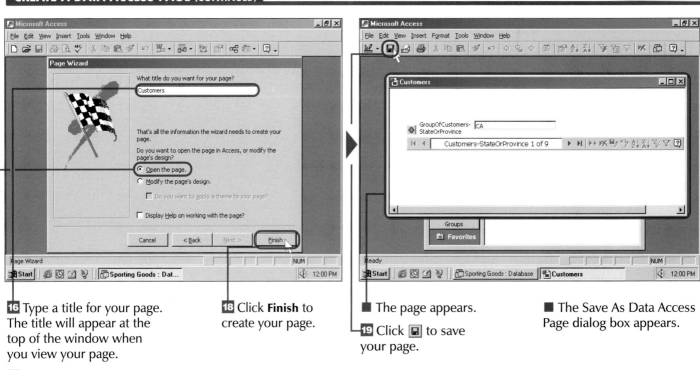

16 Type a title for your page. The title will appear at the top of the window when you view your page.

17 Click this option to open the page when you finish creating the page (○ changes to ⊙).

18 Click **Finish** to create your page.

■ The page appears.

19 Click 🖫 to save your page.

■ The Save As Data Access Page dialog box appears.

How do I open a data access page I created?

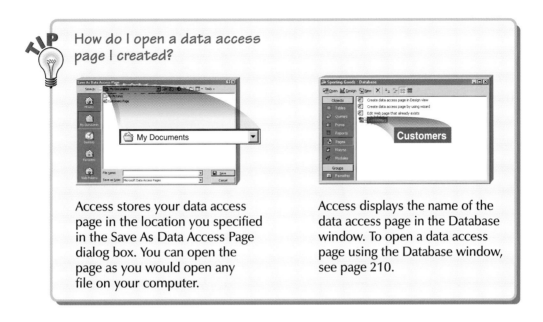

Access stores your data access page in the location you specified in the Save As Data Access Page dialog box. You can open the page as you would open any file on your computer.

Access displays the name of the data access page in the Database window. To open a data access page using the Database window, see page 210.

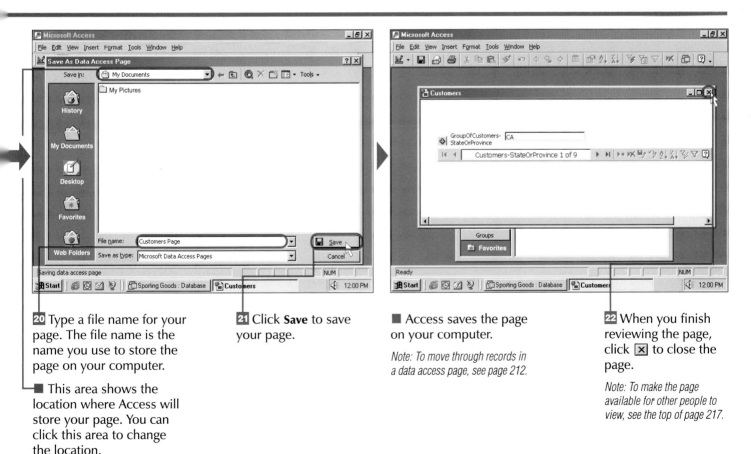

20 Type a file name for your page. The file name is the name you use to store the page on your computer.

■ This area shows the location where Access will store your page. You can click this area to change the location.

21 Click **Save** to save your page.

■ Access saves the page on your computer.

Note: To move through records in a data access page, see page 212.

22 When you finish reviewing the page, click ☒ to close the page.

Note: To make the page available for other people to view, see the top of page 217.

You can open a data access page to display its contents on your screen. This lets you review and make changes to the page.

Each time you open a data access page, Access displays the most current data from your database in the page.

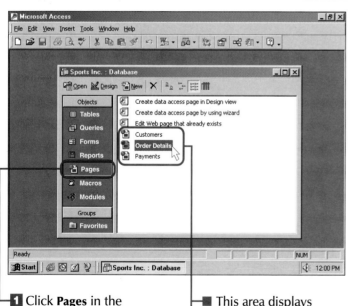

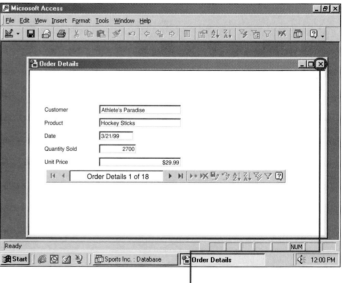

1 Click **Pages** in the Database window.

■ This area displays a list of the data access pages you have created.

2 Double-click the data access page you want to open.

■ The data access page opens. You can now review and make changes to the page.

■ When you finish working with the data access page, click ☒ to close the page.

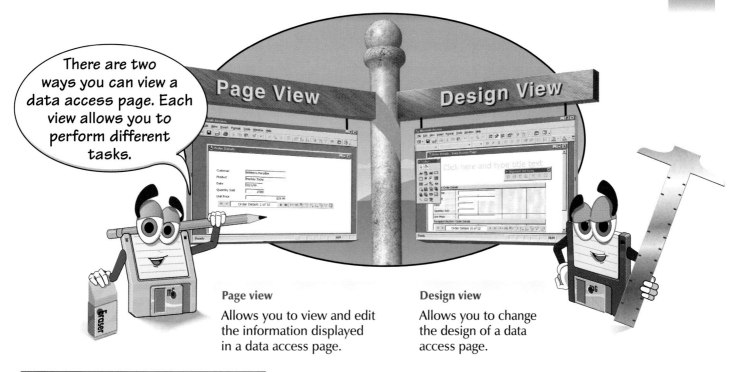

There are two ways you can view a data access page. Each view allows you to perform different tasks.

Page view

Allows you to view and edit the information displayed in a data access page.

Design view

Allows you to change the design of a data access page.

CHANGE VIEW OF DATA ACCESS PAGE

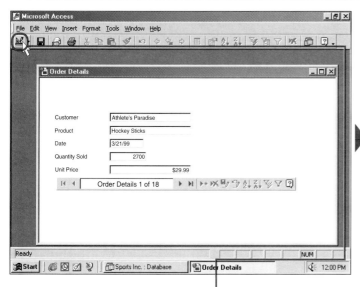

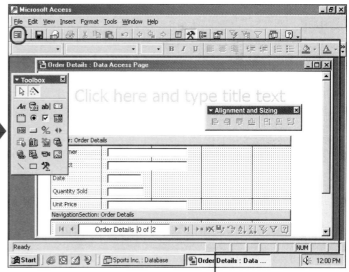

■ In this example, the data access page appears in the Page view.

1 Click to display the data access page in the Design view.

■ The data access page appears in the Design view.

■ The View button changes to . You can click the View button to quickly switch between the Page () and Design () views.

You can move through the records in a data access page to review and edit information.

MOVE THROUGH RECORDS

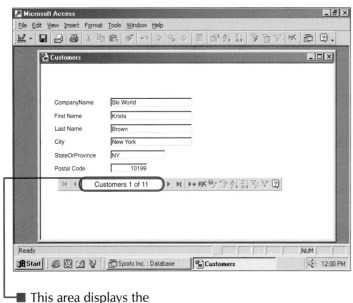

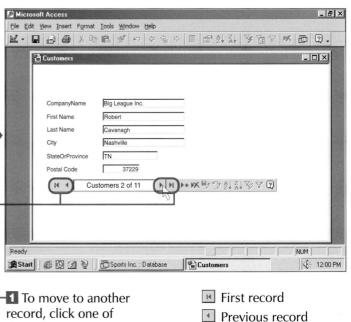

■ This area displays the number of the current record and the total number of records.

1 To move to another record, click one of these buttons.

|◄ First record

◄ Previous record

► Next record

►| Last record

Can I edit the data in my data access page?

Yes. When you change the data in a data access page, Access will also change the data in the table you used to create the page.

If you chose to group data when you created your data access page, you cannot edit the data in the page.

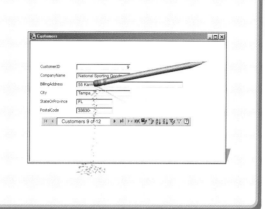

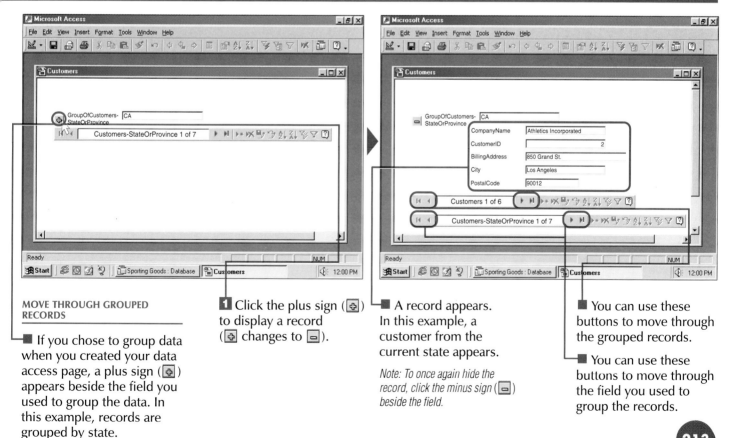

MOVE THROUGH GROUPED RECORDS

■ If you chose to group data when you created your data access page, a plus sign (⊞) appears beside the field you used to group the data. In this example, records are grouped by state.

1 Click the plus sign (⊞) to display a record (⊞ changes to ⊟).

■ A record appears. In this example, a customer from the current state appears.

Note: To once again hide the record, click the minus sign (⊟) beside the field.

■ You can use these buttons to move through the grouped records.

■ You can use these buttons to move through the field you used to group the records.

Access offers many ready-to-use designs, called themes, that you can use to enhance the appearance of your data access page.

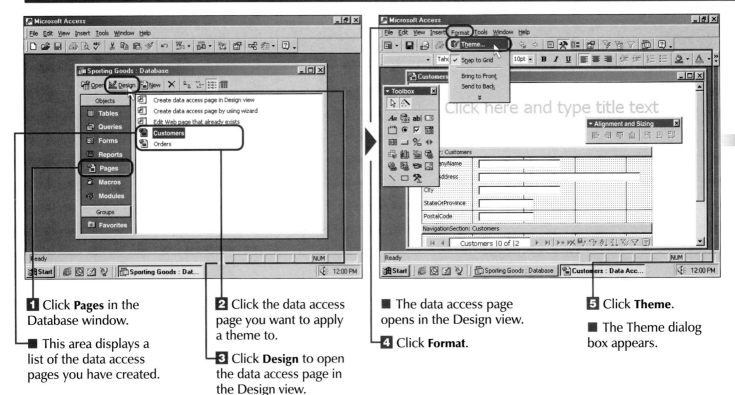

1 Click **Pages** in the Database window.

■ This area displays a list of the data access pages you have created.

2 Click the data access page you want to apply a theme to.

3 Click **Design** to open the data access page in the Design view.

■ The data access page opens in the Design view.

4 Click **Format**.

5 Click **Theme**.

■ The Theme dialog box appears.

Why didn't a sample of the theme I selected appear?

If a sample of the theme you selected does not appear, the theme is not installed on your computer. To install the theme, insert the CD-ROM disc you used to install Access into your CD-ROM drive. Then click **Install**.

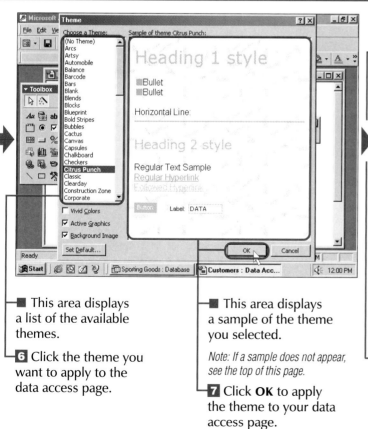

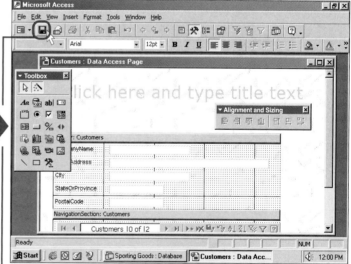

■ This area displays a list of the available themes.

6 Click the theme you want to apply to the data access page.

■ This area displays a sample of the theme you selected.

Note: If a sample does not appear, see the top of this page.

7 Click **OK** to apply the theme to your data access page.

■ The data access page displays the theme you selected.

8 Click 🖫 to save the theme.

■ To remove a theme, repeat steps **1** to **8**, selecting **(No Theme)** in step **6**.

SAVE A DATABASE OBJECT AS A WEB PAGE

You can save a table, query, form or report as a Web page. This lets you place the database object on the Internet or your company's intranet.

An intranet is a small version of the Internet within a company.

The Web page you create will not update to display changes you make to data in your database. If you want your Web page to always display the most current data, see page 204 to create a data access page.

SAVE A DATABASE OBJECT AS A WEB PAGE

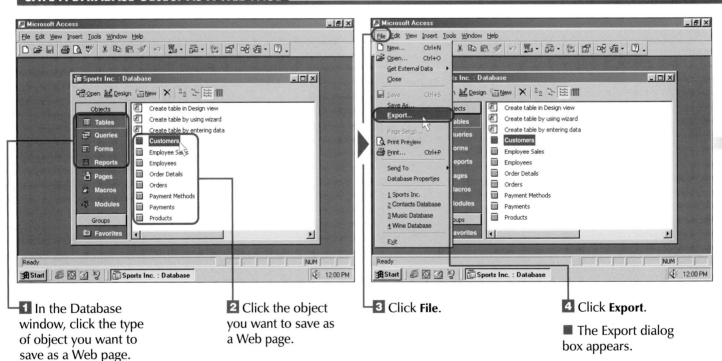

1 In the Database window, click the type of object you want to save as a Web page.

2 Click the object you want to save as a Web page.

3 Click **File**.

4 Click **Export**.

■ The Export dialog box appears.

How do I make my Web page available for other people to view?

To make a Web page available on the Internet or your company's intranet, you need to transfer the page to a Web server. A Web server is a computer that stores Web pages.

Once you publish a Web page on a Web server, the page will be available for other people to view. For more information on publishing a Web page, contact your network administrator or Internet service provider.

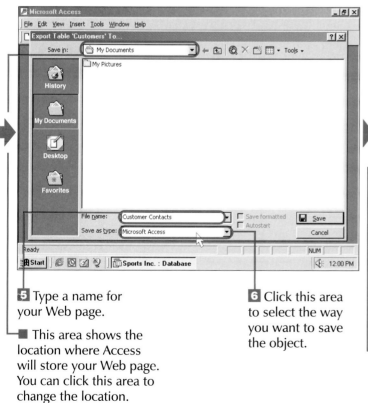

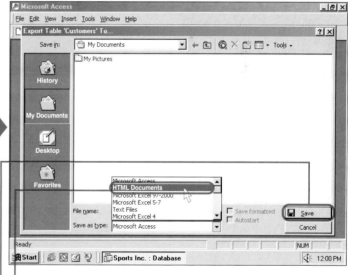

5 Type a name for your Web page.

■ This area shows the location where Access will store your Web page. You can click this area to change the location.

6 Click this area to select the way you want to save the object.

7 Click **HTML Documents** to save the object as a Web page.

8 Click **Save**.

Note: If the HTML Output Options dialog box appears, click **OK** to continue.

■ Access creates your Web page and stores the page on your computer. You can open the Web page as you would open any file on your computer. You cannot open the Web page from within Access.

INDEX

A

Access. *See also specific subject or feature*
    documents. *See* databases; forms; pages; queries;
     reports; tables
    exit, 23
    overview, 4-5
    start, 11
add
    autoformats to forms, 130-131
    fields
        description, 73
        to tables, 48
    records
        to forms, 126
        to tables, 60
    tables to queries, 147
    themes to data access pages, 214-215
    validation rules, 86-87
allow zero length strings, 84-85
And condition
    in forms, 142-143
    in queries, 168-169
appearance of objects, change, 31
apply themes to data access pages, 214-215
asterisk (*), wildcard in queries, 165
AutoForm Wizard, create forms using, 110-111
autoformats, apply to forms, 130-131
AutoNumber
    data types, 75
    for primary keys, 103
AutoReport Wizard, create reports using, 186-188
Avg, calculate
    in queries, 152-153
    in reports, 182-183

B

between, criteria, 165
blank databases, create, 18-19
browse through
    fields in tables, 52-53
    pages in reports, 190
    records
        on data access pages, 212-213
        in forms, 123
        in tables, 52-53
buttons, toolbar, display names, 22

C

calculations, perform
    in queries, 152-153, 170-171
    in reports, 182-183
cancel changes
    in forms, 125
    in tables, 57
cells
    in forms, replace data in, 125
    in tables
        copy or move data in, 58-59
        replace data, 57
        select, 55
        zoom into, 62
changes, undo
    in forms, 125
    in tables, 57
click, using mouse, 10
close
    Access, 23
    forms, 122
    objects, 31
    Print Preview, 197
    queries, 158
    reports, 189
    tables, 44
Columnar
    forms, create, 110-111
    reports, create, 186-188
columns. *See also* fields
    lookup, create, 92-95
    width, change in tables, 45
commands, select
    using menus, 20-21
    using toolbars, 22
conditions. *See also* criteria
    find records in queries using, 166-167, 168-169
copy
    data, in tables, 58-59
    vs. move, 59
count records, in queries, 153
create
    data access pages, 204-209
    databases
        blank, 18-19
        using Database Wizard, 12-17
    forms
        using AutoForm, 110-111
        using Form Wizard, 112-115, 116-121

INDEX

OVER 6 MILLION

OTHER 3-D Visual SERIES

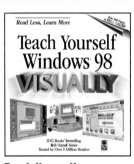
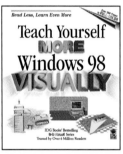
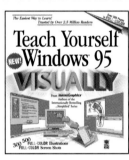

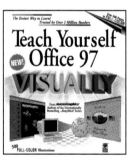

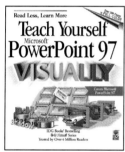
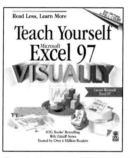

ORDER FORM

IDG BOOKS ®

TRADE & INDIVIDUAL ORDERS

Phone: **(800) 762-2974**
or **(317) 596-5200**
(8 a.m.–6 p.m., CST, weekdays)
FAX : **(800) 550-2747**
or **(317) 596-5692**

EDUCATIONAL ORDERS & DISCOUNTS

Phone: **(800) 434-2086**
(8:30 a.m.–5:00 p.m., CST, weekdays)
FAX : **(317) 596-5499**

CORPORATE ORDERS FOR 3-D VISUAL™ SERIES

Phone: **(800) 469-6616**
(8 a.m.–5 p.m., EST, weekdays)
FAX : **(905) 890-9434**

Qty	ISBN	Title	Price	Total

Shipping & Handling Charges

	Description	First book	Each add'l. book	Total
Domestic	Normal	$4.50	$1.50	$
	Two Day Air	$8.50	$2.50	$
	Overnight	$18.00	$3.00	$
International	Surface	$8.00	$8.00	$
	Airmail	$16.00	$16.00	$
	DHL Air	$17.00	$17.00	$

Subtotal _____

CA residents add
applicable sales tax _____

IN, MA and MD
residents add
5% sales tax _____

IL residents add
6.25% sales tax _____

RI residents add
7% sales tax _____

TX residents add
8.25% sales tax _____

Shipping _____

Total _____

Ship to:

Name_____

Address_____

Company_____

City/State/Zip_____

Daytime Phone_____

Payment: ☐ Check to IDG Books (US Funds Only)
   ☐ Visa ☐ Mastercard ☐ American Express

Card # _____ Exp. _____ Signature_____

***maranGraphics*™**